POPULAR GOVERNMENT

POPULAR GOVERNMENT

Its Essence,
Its Permanence
and Its Perils

William Howard Taft

With a new introduction by **Sidney A. Pearson, Jr.**

Transaction Publishers
New Brunswick (U.S.A.) and London (U.K.)

Library of Congress Catalog Number: 2009000231
ISBN: 978-1-4128-1044-9
Printed in the United States of America

Library of Congress Cataloging-in-Publication Data

Taft, William H. (William Howard), 1857-1930
    Popular government : its essence, its permanence and its perils /
    William Howard Taft, with a new introduction by Sidney A. Pearson.
        p. cm.
    Originally published: New Haven, CT : Yale University Press. 1913.
    Includes bibliographical references and index.
    ISBN 978-1-4128-1044-9 (alk. paper)
        1. United States--Politics and government--Philosophy. I. Title.

JK1726.T34 2009
320.973--dc22
                                                                2009000231

CONTENTS

INTRODUCTION TO THE
TRANSACTION EDITION[1]

William Howard Taft's political resume is impressive; he served as the twenty-third president of the United States from 1909-1913 and as Chief Justice of the Supreme Court from 1921-1930. He is the only person to have held the highest office in two of the three branches of American government. Unfortunately for his general reputation as president, his presidency was sandwiched between the towering presidential personalities of Theodore Roosevelt from 1901-1909, for whom Taft served as Vice President from 1905-1909, and Woodrow Wilson from 1913-1921. To top it off, he finished third in the three-way presidential election of 1912 to both Roosevelt and Wilson while amassing the lowest popular vote total for any presidential candidate representing one of the two major parties since the invention of the two-party system. Whatever personal and political virtues might be ascribed to Taft, no one has ever argued that he could compete with either of these two presidents in terms of charismatic personality. He did not particularly like retail politics and was a far happier while serving as Chief Justice of the Supreme Court than during his tenure as president. In addition, both Roosevelt and Wilson have been viewed through the lens of progressive historiography, the dominant tradition in American historiography, as heralding the birth of the modern presidency. It is this perspective which has made Taft appear to be no more than a conservative, if not reactionary, counterpoint to the progressive argument that the presidency is the heart and soul of the American political system.[2] Why bother to read someone irrelevant to the development of modern American politics?

But it is precisely because Taft is not associated with the modern presidency that makes him worth revisiting. The modern presidency has come to be seen as increasingly problematic by persons of the most diverse political views and on all sides of the political spectrum. Students of American politics are not only obliged to ask "why this does seems to be so?" but also to offer some account of "why" the dominant progressive view of the modern presidency itself has become so problematic. Taft, his administration and his political thought, is a good place to look to try to unravel some of theoretical problems associated with the modern presidency. While we should always be mindful of the specific politics of his administration, the core problems associated with the modern presidency require an inquiry into the foundational principles of the presidency itself. We shall not be remiss, therefore, if we begin our discussion of Taft's presidency by focusing on his foundational arguments about the nature of the presidency and then the larger constitutional context in which all such arguments over institutions take place. We start with his post-presidential writings in which he had an opportunity to reflect on the ideas and politics surrounding him in the midst of what we rightly call the Progressive Era.

Taft's own interpretation of his presidency and of the office in general, published as *Our Chief Magistrate and His Powers* (1916), is typically treated as a footnote to the presidency of the Republican Roosevelt. While Taft was not a gifted politician as were Roosevelt and Wilson, his post-presidential reflections on the nature of American government are among the most thoughtful of any ex-president. In it he wrote from a perspective that is absolutely unique in American thought. His constitutional views are especially pertinent in the wake of the post-Vietnam and post-Watergate arguments over the nature of executive powers and when the liberal-progressive tradition of constitutional interpretation has become more controversial than at any time since its origins at the turn of the twentieth century.[3] The return to a reconsideration of Taft's views on both executive power and constitutional interpretation is therefore in order. But such reconsideration is not rooted in a nostalgic wish to return to another time and place of constitutional interpretation: it may be too late for that however attractive it may seem on the surface. Rather it is to try to better understand how and why the Progressive Movement marks one of the major turning points in American political thought and to better understand that turning point from the vantage point of one of its most perspicuous contemporary critics. It is prompted first and foremost by a concern over the nature of the American regime. How important are the founding principles of the regime both for our self-understanding as a people and for our daily exercise of citizenship in the Republic? Are the founding principles something to be overcome in order to realize what Herbert Croly once called "the promise of American life"? Or are these same principles the basis for a decent form of popular government that we abandon at our collective peril? These are the fundamental questions addressed by Taft in *Popular Government* (1913) and they remain our questions a century later.

The view of Taft as a run-of-the-mill president is not entirely mistaken, although it has been exaggerated by more than one historian. This academic judgment is rooted in the notion that Roosevelt and Wilson are convenient reference points for the rise of the modern presidency, and Taft does not fit the liberal-progressive profile of what the modern chief executive should be. The bias of most presidential scholars has always been toward an activist presidency and a "conservative activist" seems to be an oxymoron. But it is precisely the criteria liberal-progressives have used to define the presidency and interpret American democracy that is the issue here. Activism to what end? Are some ends destructive of the foundations of a republican political science that is the heart of the founders' defense of constitutional government? The general intellectual structure of the progressive interpretation of American democracy in general and the presidency in particular needs to be rethought and reinterpreted as the consequences of the progressive assault on the Founders' constitutional principles have become more evident.

A good place to begin thinking about the political philosophy of the Progressives is in the work of William Howard Taft, both because he was a contemporary of Roosevelt and Wilson and because his broad ranging critique of both the theory and practice of liberal-progressivism remains instructive today. The constitutional foundations of his critique of the emerging liberal-progressive science of politics deserve to be considered independently of his service as president. And there is more to Taft's understanding of the principles of American government than the all too facile tendency to simply label him a "conservative" or personalize his critique of Roosevelt and let it go at that. On the one hand, there is an obvious sense in which "conservative" is an appropriate term, although he also referred to himself as a "progressive." But there is more to Taft's political philosophy than the dismissive connotations the use of this term too often implies. Indeed, the use of such terms more often conceal than illuminate serious political analysis as an inquiry into Taft's constitutional understanding will reveal.

Popular Government and Progressive Political Science: The Importance of Foundational Arguments

Theodore Roosevelt's "stewardship" theory is rightly regarded as one of the first philosophical expressions of the modern presidency. It is worth quoting here because so much of Taft's defense of a more traditional presidency may be properly understood as a critique of Roosevelt and what his stewardship theory represented. Roosevelt wrote in his autobiography, "The most important factor in getting the right spirit in my administration ... was my insistence upon the theory that the executive power was limited only by specific restrictions and prohibitions appearing in the Constitution, or imposed by Congress under its Constitutional powers. My view was that every executive officer, and above all every executive officer in high position, was a steward of the people bound actively and affirmatively to do all he could for the people, and not to content himself with the negative merit of keeping his talents undamaged in a napkin."[4] The view neatly captured Roosevelt's personality and revealed why, in practical terms, he was such an effective and popular president. But it also raises troubling theoretical questions about not only his constitutional judgment, but also whether or not the Founders' Constitution remains adequate for the politics in the modern world: the emerging liberal-progressive tradition Roosevelt embodied thought that it was not, while Taft thought that it was. This quarrel has been a permanent feature of American political life ever since. Taft took it for granted that his was more or less the same as the republican political science of *The Federalist* and did not require further elaboration than simply to note it as a fact.

Taft's rejoinder to Roosevelt's remarks has been routinely quoted by almost every study of the presidency written since the initial exchange took place. It is an impressive though brief argument on executive powers under an original understanding of the Constitution that owes more to Hamilton than is commonly assumed by those scholars who only read the excerpt from Taft and not the whole of his thought. As Carey McWilliams has observed of Taft's work, he makes his case against Roosevelt "without rancor and in terms of principles, as if indicating the issues involved transcend personalities."[5] It is a fair assessment. Taft wrote, "The true view of the Executive function is, as I conceive it, that the President can exercise no power which cannot be fairly and reasonably traced to some specific grant of power or justly implied and included within such express grant as proper and necessary to its exercise.... There is no undefined residuum of power which he can exercise because it seems to him to be in the public interest.... The grants of Executive power are necessarily in general terms in order not to embarrass the Executive within the field of action plainly marked for him, but his jurisdiction must be justified and vindicated by affirmative constitutional or statutory provision, or it does not exist."[6] But while it is appropriate to see this passage as a critique of Roosevelt (Taft is absolutely explicit on this point), there is more here than a personal critique involved. We can gain a broader perspective by considering Woodrow Wilson rather than Theodore Roosevelt as the real philosophical opponent of Taft. The reason is that while Roosevelt never developed an elaborate constitutional defense of his theory of executive power, Wilson made such a defense the center of his mature, pre-presidential writing. And like Wilson, Taft was an interpreter of the Constitution with formidable skills in foundational reasoning. We will therefore gain a better understanding of Taft if we compare him first with Wilson then with Roosevelt.

The progressive tradition tends to ascribe Taft's argument to an outmoded "Whig" interpretation of government, to borrow the term used by Woodrow Wilson.[7] But there is more to Taft's argument than can be summed up in terms such as "Whig," "strict construction," or even "conservative" as that last term is generally applied. Edward Corwin noted as early as 1940 that Taft's constitutional understanding had been fundamentally misunderstood by those progressive scholars tutored by Woodrow Wilson's *Constitutional Government* (1908).[8] The progressive reason for the misunderstanding, or perhaps mischaracterization, of Taft can be traced to the foundational arguments of the liberal- progressive tradition of political science.

The liberal-progressive tradition was at war with the Founders' science of politics, represented most forcefully and eloquently in *The Federalist*. The aim of the liberal-progressive movement articulated by Wilson and others was to impose on the Constitution a "newer" science of politics. This new science of politics used Darwin as the dynamic model of scientific analysis rather than what they saw as the static model of Newton that they thought dominated the Founders' political science. A few remarks on the liberal-progressive science of politics are required here in order to better understand how and where Taft fits into this debate over the nature of the American constitutional system.

Woodrow Wilson's *Constitutional Government* is rightly regarded as the paradigmatic representation of the liberal-progressive tradition; it embodies the foundational arguments of modern liberal-progressivism over constitutional interpretation that have been a hallmark of that tradition ever since. According to Wilson, true constitutional government "evolves" through at least four distinct stages according to the logic of Darwin, during which true democracy is not reached until the fourth and final stage of development. The American Founders were locked into a Newtonian understanding of science that affirmed fixed principles: when they applied this Newtonian science to politics the result was a natural rights argument that assumed a rationally moral and fixed universe as their foundational argument. As Wilson wrote, "In our own day, whenever we discuss the structure or development of anything, whether in nature or society, we consciously or unconsciously follow Mr. Darwin."[9] This means that any practical problem with the American Constitution, such as how much power rightly belongs to the president in a separated system, is at bottom a philosophical problem: a problem the Founders got wrong. They got the problem wrong first and foremost because their science of politics is based on fixed principles that have locked the regime into what Wilson described as the third stage of a system not yet fully developed as a democracy. The constitutional debates in *The Federalist,* for example, are based on republican principles appropriate to the third stage of constitutional development but not to the fourth stage of true democracy. In this sense, the founding arguments are scientifically inadequate either to explain or to guide a modern and democratic form of government. To paraphrase Herbert Croly, the democratic promise of American life has yet to be realized.

The theoretical as well as the practical problem of building a true democracy merged, Wilson thought, in his project to replace the Founders' science of politics, built on a foundation of natural rights, separation of powers, and the like with a more scientific science of politics following Darwin rather than Newton. Constitutional government, on this new scientific foundation, had no fixed principles of interpretation and the natural rights reasoning of the Declaration of Independence was rejected outright. Although Wilson did not use the term, his work helped to establish what has been called the "living constitution" school of thought. And while it may be true to say that Wilson probably did not intend his arguments to result in the constitutional relativism that it has, his Hegelian conception of historical progress did not provide a new foundation for political science as much as it has undermined the prospects for any foundation in the first place.[10] More will be said of this point later.

It is important to understand this historicized argument of the liberal-progressive tradition in order to understand Taft's response. If the Constitution evolves over time and therefore has no fixed meaning, it is difficult to understand why we would even need a written Constitution in the first place.[11] Wilson's attempt to build a new foundational argument for political science based on historical evolution turns out to be no founda-

tion at all. The British Constitution, which Wilson
and most others in the liberal-progressive tradition much admired, is unwritten and consists of
whatever laws are passed by parliament. Under
the British system, the problem of an unconstitutional law does not arise—certainly not in the
sense of American government—because the British Constitution is whatever parliament says it
is at any particular time. But it is not really the
British Constitution that need concern us here.
What does need to be pointed out is that within
the liberal-progressive idea of how the United
States Constitution evolves it is not obvious on the
face of it what, if anything, might be considered
"unconstitutional." The very idea that anything
might be unconstitutional rests on the implicit notion that the Constitution has at least some fixed
principles of interpretation that can be rationally
understood, what Alexander Hamilton in *The
Federalist* referred to as "primary truths or first
principles" upon which all subsequent political
reasoning depends (*Fed. 31*). It is the inability of
the liberal-progressive tradition to ground its political science on fixed principles that has tended
to make so much of its attempt to interpret the
Constitution, either from academia or the judiciary, so intellectually incoherent so much of the
time. Occasional attempts to declare something

unconstitutional, however valid that something might be in a particular case, will always appear opportunistic or inconsistent with earlier arguments, and recourse to anything as vague as "evolution" does nothing to clarify the attempt. There is no foundation to provide answers because everything is in flux: there are only questions when practical politicians need answers.

Foundational arguments are essential for political science because, first and foremost, political science is a practical as opposed to a theoretical science. Any argument that really provides a foundation for subsequent reasoning is one that will be, as the Declaration of Independence affirms, built on "self evident Truths": that is, precisely because it is a foundation it is not an object of inquiry, but rather the basis upon which all subsequent reasoning can proceed. Without a foundation, it seems doubtful that any form of reasoning about anything of significance can take place. The purpose of foundational reasoning in political science, as works from Aristotle to Tocqueville have explained, is to develop knowledge that political actors, "those who direct society," can use in their political activities. This point is as true for Aristotle as it is for Machiavelli. Foundational arguments will always tend to be expressed in general terms but that does not mean they have no practical significance: without a foundation that can be rationally articulated, political science is impossible. Furthermore, what we refer to as foundational arguments from Aristotle through Tocqueville, which covers a considerable diversity of thought, were commonly based on a concept of human nature that had certain fixed limits. Among other things, the Darwinian argument undermined the notion that human nature was in any real sense fixed. If human nature was not fixed, then fixed principles of political science did not make much sense either.

But reason itself seems to require some sort of foundation, as the absence of a foundation tends to send so many attempts at reasoning into seemingly endless rounds of epistemological inquiry: what do we know and how do we know it? Such a political science has real difficulty ever arriving at the sort of practical knowledge that is the basis for how to act in ordinary politics in the first place. The liberal-progressive attack on foundational reasoning in virtually any form as "authoritarian," such as the natural rights argument at the founding of the American regime, is what has set scholarship in the Wilsonian mold against regime principles as they were understood by the Founders.[12] Taft's constitutional reasoning, as we shall see, included an explicit critique of the liberal-progressives on the point of fixed principles of human nature. In so doing it is not necessary to show that Taft agreed with every point in *The Federalist* or with any particular person we may associate with the founding arguments of the polity: it will be sufficient to show how he was in substantial agreement to the extent that he shared the same paradigmatic understanding of regime analysis.

Taft's defense of the Founders' concept of republican citizenship is at the heart of *Popular Government* and the work as a whole is unlikely to be understood until and unless we understand Taft's discussion of citizenship. Without such a foundation argument regarding citizen behavior, he makes explicit his view that constitutional reasoning in the broad sense of the term would be impossible. At one level, that reasoning is equally evident in his *Our Chief Magistrate and His Powers* written in response to Roosevelt's open-ended "stewardship" theory of executive power. It seems fair in this context to note that we may better understand the particular arguments so oft quoted in *Our Chief Magistrate* if we begin with his more general arguments less quoted in *Popular Government*. There is more to his understanding the Constitution as the foundation for first principles than his explication of executive power under Article II alone. As Taft understood the liberal-progressive challenge, it in turn requires an inquiry into the meaning of the Constitution as a whole. Such a discussion at this point cannot take up Taft's constitutional reasoning and interpretation when he served as Chief Justice of the Supreme Court, but it can focus on what we might call the interregnum period, after he left the presidency and before he became Chief Justice of the Supreme Court.

The Foundational Argument of Popular Government

Paradoxically, the very qualities that limited Taft's success as a president made him a superior *student* of the presidency.[13] He did not particularly enjoy the day-to-day business of politics in the way Roosevelt did, but his sense of a legalistic detachment from politics did give him just the right perspective to combine broad theory with personal experience in a way that is uncommon of one who has held the office of Chief Executive. No other ex-president has written as systematically about how and where the president fits into the constitutional system and the broad principles of the Constitution itself as has Taft. Again, his reputation in this regard among scholars has suffered in part by viewing his administration through the lens of liberal-progressive scholarship. As Stephen Skowronek, a later student of the presidency has insightfully observed, after Taft was elected in his own right in 1908 he faced an impossible task that colored both his and later scholarly arguments on the Constitution. He notes that Roosevelt's administration had strengthened the liberal-progressives and legitimized not merely their *ends* but their *means* as well. When Taft faithfully tried to follow Roosevelt's reform agenda he sought to do so through existing institutional means, only to discover that the liberal-progressive reformers no longer regarded existing institutional means as legitimate.[14] Taft confronted this problem head-on after he left office in 1913 in a series of lectures delivered at Yale University and published that same year under the title *Popular Government: Its Essence, Its Permanence, and Its Perils.* The title was nicely chosen: it reflected a concern broader than merely executive power studied in isolation from the rest of the Constitution.

Popular Government begins with an inquiry into Preamble to the Constitution when Taft asks what do we really mean by "We the People of the United States"? It is the starting point for Taft because citizenship in a republican form of government is the lynchpin of his constitutional defense: it is the point where constitutional theory meets constitutional practice in a popular form of government. In drawing our attention to the issue of citizenship, his work deliberately makes the point that the moral calculus of popular government, embodied in the term "citizen," is more important as a foundation than any historicized political calculus divorced from such concerns. His defense of women's suffrage, for example, is illustrative of how he thought about practical issues: "women should be accorded the privilege, and given the duty, of voting, not because they have an inherent and inalienable right to vote, but because by giving them the franchise, their own welfare or that of the whole body of the people will thereby be promoted."[15] The right to vote entails corresponding obligations and should be seen as what Tocqueville called "self-interest, rightly understood": both the individual as well as the collective good are served by an extension of the franchise. It is not necessary here to engage in a wide-ranging discussion of each point Taft makes in these lectures on practical issues such as voting rights for women. We only need to illuminate Taft's thought and to grasp his critique of the liberal-progressive tradition. And while Taft does not specifically single-out Woodrow Wilson's constitutionalism, it seems clear from the outset that Taft is thoroughly familiar with at least the philosophic thrust of Wilson's argument.

The Preamble to the Constitution does not lend itself to statutory interpretation, but it is part of the foundational argument of the Founders' Constitution upon which, as Hamilton thought, subsequent reasoning depends.[16] Understanding the Preamble is the starting point of Constitutional understanding because it is antecedent to the republican principles of the founding as opposed to the democratic principles that were explicitly rejected in *The Federalist*. And Taft demonstrates that he well appreciates the distinction the Founders made between these *two* forms of popular government: one form was democratic and the other form republican. Democratic government was defined as the rule of the many through direct participation, simple majority rule that concentrated power, and was more appropriate, or at least more possible, in a small territory. Republican government was defined as the rule of the many but was representative in form, divided the categories of general political power into distinct institutions, and was appropriate for a larger, more diverse territorial state. Both were "popular" in the sense that they rested on the consent of the governed, but each also rested on different founding principles of government. "Popular government," according to Taft, "may properly be defined to be a government established and maintained by the authority of the people."[17] It was a definition that included both democratic and republican forms in theory, while in the American practice it meant a republican form. That American government has changed over time, with respect to such things as the expansion of suffrage and the emancipation of slaves, does not suggest "evolution" away from founding principles for Taft so much as it points toward the greater realization of the natural rights foundation of the republic: "These facts do not make against government of the people as we understand it. It only shows that approval of so-called popular government is not worship of a fetish."[18] The proper expansion of foundational principles is not a repudiation of those principles.

The Constitution was explicitly republican in principle, not because it was hostile to popular government, as scholars in the liberal-progressive tradition such as Charles Beard, Herbert Croly, and Frank Goodnow, for example, had argued, but because it was an attempt to balance competing principles that could not, as *The Federalist* had argued, be reconciled by democratic principles alone; such as majority rule and minority rights. In addition, the Founders distrusted the concentration of power and defined such a concentration as the very essence of tyranny, whereas Wilson and most others in the liberal-progressive tradition saw the concentration of power as essential for the realization of true democracy: tyranny in the political science of the liberal-progressives, by implication, was the absence of fourth-stage democracy. The separation of powers for the Founders, for example, was not designed to thwart majority rule, as the liberal-progressive tradition has tended to argue, but to make institutionalized tyranny more difficult. Taft, contrary to the liberal-progressives and more in keeping with the original Founders, insisted that popular government is a means to larger ends, not an end in itself.[19] The evolutionary theory of constitutional development according to Wilson made republican government no more than a speed-bump on the road to democracy. And we can appreciate the power and the pervasiveness of the Wilsonian argument by recalling how difficult it has become since Wilson to think of democratic and republican government as representing different forms of popular government, much less to appreciate the different principles that animate their operations.

There was more involved in this argument over the fundamental forms of popular government than merely a semantic or abstract distinction: it was a practical argument about institutions appropriate for a specific form of popular government. In the Founders' scheme of constitutional government, freedom and the protection of minorities had to be combined with majority rule in an extended territory to produce a complex argument that did not easily lend themselves to the simpler idea of majority rule alone. The Wilsonian argument on constitutional development made democracy the simple end of politics rather than a means to secure the more complex ends of a republican form. Progress for Wilson meant a decisive break with the past. Indeed, the very idea that a government might have a particular "form" with its own principles was dissolved by the Darwinian notion of science. As Taft observes in the first paragraph of his Introduction, "I thought it relevant and important to discuss the proposed changes from our republican form of government to a more direct, democratic government..."[20] Taft not only knew and understood the difference between democratic and republican government, he also knew and understood the difference it makes and the problems involved in grafting principles appropriate for a democracy onto a constitution designed for a republic.

Different forms of government required different civic cultures with correspondingly different virtues of citizenship to support them. And as Madison noted at the conclusion to *Federalist 55*, "Republican government presupposes the existence of these qualities in a higher degree than any other form": rights and obligations were mutually reinforcing qualities of active citizenship. Taft's discussion of the sort of citizenship implied in the Preamble must be set against his awareness of these arguments. The liberal-progressive argument on citizenship tended to stress a group basis of politics. Citizenship rights as a consequence evolved into a group basis for rights rather than the individual basis of rights in the Madisonian conception of citizenship.[21] We can trace the break between the Founders' constitution and the Wilsonian constitution in part by considering the impact the latter had on citizenship.

"We the people" means, for Taft, "the people" in a representative system and not, for the most part, direct participation: certainly not direct participation in the Founders' sense, where the people meet in person to administer the laws. Nor, it must be said, did Wilson think of fourth-stage democracy as direct participation. But Wilson did, as did most others in the liberal-progressive tradition, think of participation as something that focused on groups rather than as something that focused on individuals: representation therefore tended to be thought of as group representation. Further, Taft insisted that the phrase "We the people" had to be tied to the cultivation of citizenship among the people. And citizenship, in turn, is a concept that transcends economic categories of people too often organized according to class—and it might be added that adding "race" and "gender" to the mix does not clarify the issue. Citizenship in this conception precluded proportional representation by groups. The democratic system of the liberal-progressive model, he wrote, makes the political science of the Founders "unsound and outworn" because of "their alleged class feeling."[22] But class consciousness destroys republican citizenship which is not restored merely because it is linked to a theory of progressive democracy. The liberal-progressive science of politics did not literally en-vision national government by town-meeting, but its relentless thrust was participatory democracy by groups even if it was vague on specifics. And it was this relentless thrust of argument insist-ing that the Constitution was undemocratic that called into question the republican principles of third-stage popular government.

The vagueness of the liberal-progressive argu-ment on how democracy was to be defined was itself a product of the Darwinian idea of evolution. This vagueness was translated into a dilemma

Taft diagnosed as the emerging problem of constitutional interpretation in the liberal-progressive model. A definition would imply fixed principles and Wilson denied the validity of a political science organized around an analysis of specific forms of government in the first place. One of the casualties of this new narrative of constitutional development as Taft saw it was that the idea that citizenship ceased to have any fixed connection to the form of government. This meant that arguments regarding democracy would be severed from any link to the republican conception of citizen obligations at the founding. Taft found the conceptual foundation of the liberal-progressive argument unconvincing. He wrote, "I do not think that this school of political philosophy will ultimately triumph."[23] The reason for its ultimate failure, Taft was convinced, would be the philosophical incompatibility of these new principles with existing constitutional institutions. The sort of citizenship required for a republic is fundamentally different than the citizenship required by a more participatory democracy. It is certainly different from the sort of citizenship envisioned by group rights that defined much of the liberal-progressive agenda. But, we might reasonably ask at this point, precisely how does the liberal-progressive notion of group rights and citizenship based on these rights pose a challenge to our understanding of citizenship in the Founders' political science? The question requires a discussion of ends and means in popular forms of government that the Wilsonian science of democracy obscures. Taft appreciated the problem as well as anyone at the time.

Republican Government and the Progressive Challenge

Understanding the distinction between ends and means is essential in both theory and practice because, as Taft put it, there are "a good many fetishes that now lie in wait for the unsophisticated reformer."[24] The constitutional incompatibility of the Wilsonian argument with the Founders' Constitution was nowhere more evident than in Taft's selection of topics for consideration. First, and perhaps foremost, is the significance of *representation* for the republican principle and *participation* for the democratic principle. Both qualities are important in a popular form of government, but each operates differently in terms of citizenship. Taft's first point of criticism of the liberal-progressive argument took up its insistence upon both democratic participation and the necessity of group representation in an extended republic such as the United States. The two principles were not easily blended and the difficulties could be seen in the reform proposals for the "Initiative," "Referendum," and "Recall." Both were attempts to graft direct participatory principles onto a republican Constitution: the Initiative as a device in which the people could by-pass the legislature and propose laws directly, the Referendum as a device whereby the people could approve or disapprove a particular legislative proposal, and the Recall as a device where the people could remove elected officials from office prior to scheduled elections. Taft pointedly asked what might we reasonably expect to happen, especially with regard to citizenship, with adoption of such popular proposals?

He begins with the observation that it is impossible to escape the proposition that we do not, in fact, have a government that includes all of the people in a literal sense. If we define democracy as a system that requires participation at all levels of operation we immediately encounter some practical problems. This becomes obvious in any discussion of the franchise: some groups participate at greater levels of activity than others. Nevertheless, he observes, "… in fixing our federal franchise we do seek to make our voters in a true sense representatives of all the people."

Enlargement of the franchise, to include women, for example, expands the authority of "the people." This is a necessary expansion because republican government as Americans understand it requires the individual consent of the governed: and here the act of voting is the most active form of consent. But we all know that not everyone who is eligible will exercise the right to vote. "What is the remedy for this?" he asks. We have only two choices: (1) compel the delinquents to vote, or (2) call on the electorate for less frequent direct political participation by a system of representation with periodic elections.[25] Taft opts for the second solution because it does not impose on the average citizen responsibilities beyond their normal interest or capacity to act responsibly. Further, the representative in the legislature represents those who did not vote as well as those who did. This is Taft's reformulation of the solution proposed by Madison when he wrote in *The Federalist*, that too frequent appeals to the people "would carry an implication of some defect in the government, (and) frequent appeals would in great measure deprive the government of that veneration, which time bestows on everything, and without which perhaps the wisest and freest governments would not possess the requisite stability" (*Fed. 49*).

In effect, if not necessarily by intention, a political system that imposes too many obligations on citizens will lead to neglect of those obligations by increasing numbers of those citizens. The practical result will be a form of government by those citizens who do vote and the government will then become representative of an active minority in which the more passive majority is neglected. The group basis of politics thus carries with it the seeds of corruption of the republican form of government. "It is altogether an error to assume that a man who neglects his own political duties is only injuring himself. He is injuring everybody who has a right to the exercise by him of his intelligence and experience in the decision of the questions presented to the electorate. It is a just cause of complaint against the laws if they provide electoral duties so heavy that they necessarily discourage his political activity."[26] It is for this reason that Taft thinks a form of representation better supports a popular form of government than does direct participation. The republican government the Founders bequeathed to us is a system in which "the average intelligence of the electorate may exert its proper influence at the polls, and that a system which wearies the mass of voters and keeps them from the polls is condemned by that fact."[27] In Taft's formulation of the issue, it is

citizenship combined with institutionalized electoral participation, and not group participation
or group representation alone, that defines the
nature of a democratic constitutional process.

Here it must be noted that Taft explicitly
defends what has come to be referred to as a
theory of representation commonly associated
with Edmund Burke. The argument of Burke
on representation generally takes the view that
the popularly elected representative brings to
the affairs of government his moral character
as well as his independent knowledge of public
affairs; the voter elects each in some measure
in the same person, and it is this independence
on the part of the representative that makes
its influence felt at the point of public acts both
legislative and executive. Taft observed, "We the
people" typically desire the common good but "are
generally lacking in the knowledge and practical
experience to devise a practical measure to secure
it. It would seem wise on our part to employ in
such matters men who have special knowledge
and experience..."[28] As government increases its
functions, as it has since Jefferson's day when the
function of government was primarily that of a
police system, the need for specialized knowledge
in administration has increased, not diminished.
"This is a system of representative democracy, in

the sense that the people ultimately govern, but they make the government effective by the use of consent agents whom they elect as their representatives."[29] And since most of these specialists exercise their expertise as part of the exercise of the administrative function of government, it is appropriate that most of these specialists will receive their appointments from the executive branch of government. If this seems to increase executive power at the expense of the legislative power, it is only an appearance: what is involved is an increase in the functions of modern government caused by economic changes within the culture as a whole.

Here it must be said that Burke does not usually speak for the theory of representation typically associated with the Founders, although there is some ambiguity on this point. James Madison in *Federalist 55* and *56* does suggest that at the highest level, representation is more than the representation of specific interests and encompasses the whole of the polity. James Madison, in his discussion of the House, observed, "As it is essential to liberty that the government in general, should have a common interest with the people; so it is particularly essential that the branch of government under consideration, should have immediate dependence on, and an intimate sympathy with the people" (*Fed. 52*). He understood the electoral connection but Madison wanted constitutional space between the people and their representatives so that the elected representatives could do their work and allow representatives to also represent the Constitution as a whole. It is in the Senate and in the President, however, where the longer tenures in office would most support the sort of independent expertise Taft quoting Burke favored. In any case, the liberal-progressive argument on representative of group interests was linked to their view of parties as representative of group interests, a view that later became the "responsible party" school of thought. Taft did not deny that parties were composed of groups, but he did affirm that the first responsibility of parties was not to these groups but to the Constitution defended in *The Federalist* and by John Marshall's Supreme Court.

What changes in part the Founders' conceptual understanding of representation, for Taft however, is the necessity for political parties in a modern system of popular government. The Founders' Constitution was not designed to accommodate political parties, although Madison reconciled himself to parties even before the election of Jefferson in 1800. And reformed parties were at the heart of specific proposals advanced by liberal-progressive scholars such as Woodrow Wilson and Frank Goodnow. Goodnow, in his enormously influential *Politics and Administration* (1900), wrote that the failure of the American party system was rooted in the Constitution. The remedy was either to change the Constitution, which he doubted was realistically feasible, or change political parties in such a way that the Constitution would operate differently than it does. He wrote, "The party in the American political system has to do what in other political systems is devolved upon the formal governmental organization. But the reason that the party does this work is to be found in the character of the governmental system itself."[30] In order to change the function of parties, Goodnow argued, it would be necessary to change the fundamental constitutional structure of the government. What came to be called the "responsible party" school in American politics became one of the staple arguments of the liberal-progressive tradition.[31] Taft recognized the validity of Goodnow's starting point regarding parties, but rejected his conclusions for many of the reasons discussed above. But on the issue of parties, Taft was well positioned to offer some original views of his own.

The addition of political parties to the Founders' Constitution complicates Taft's defense of the Founders in his quarrel with the emerging liberal-progressive critique of the Constitution, but does not alter its foundation. James Ceaser, for example, has argued that the invention of the modern two-party system after the four-way election of 1824, largely by Martin Van Buren, was a necessary invention designed to preserve the integrity of the presidential selection process by protecting the separation of powers.[32] Paradoxically, although the Constitution was not designed to accommodate parties, parties were necessary to preserve its original design regarding the independent selection of the president from legislative interference. On the face of it, Taft would appear to agree with the Wilson-Goodnow idea that somehow political parties would have to become more responsible if government itself were to be more responsible to the electorate.

The point of difference between Taft and the others was whether this could or should be done within the existing constitutional framework, or would the foundational arguments of the Constitution have to be changed to accommodate reform agenda advanced by responsible party advocates. Taft opted for the notion that the parties would have to operate within the existing Constitution if they were to operate responsibly. And this meant, among other things, accepting the idea that rights belong to individuals and not to groups. Parties owed a responsibility not only to the electorate, but to the Constitution as well. "In a proper system of party government, the members of each party must agree on certain main doctrines in respect to governmental policy..."[33] Beyond some policies, however, the ultimate obligation of each representative was to the Constitution that transcended any particular policy just as citizenship should transcend a particular group identity. We only need to note here that such a view of political parties was an anathema to those reformers who saw the function of parties primarily as agents to present policy options to the public and not to defend constitutional principles. Indeed, the notion that parties should defend the constitutional principles of the founders was in many ways at the heart of the liberal-progressive critique of traditional parties.

The responsible party school of government, Taft observes matter-of-factly, arose in response to major social changes, especially in the aftermath of the Civil War. He shared many of their concerns over the corruption of the political system. The growth of "The Commercial Spirit" corrupted more than one state capitol and aroused the "indignant spirit of the people" who rightly demanded change: "That the occasion for a general alarm was justified, no one who has studied the situation can deny."[34] Taft did not deny that the corruption of government by powerful economic interests required specific legislation beyond the scope that the Founders would or could have anticipated. The mobilization of the public under these circumstances may lead to some excesses in legislative remedies, he thought, but the "advantage derived from their quickened conscience, however, is worth all the incidental mistakes or injustices that may be done, before the sobering effect of experience produces a reaction carrying conditions back, not to the abuses of the old, but to that point where the original movement might wisely have ended."[35] But whereas Taft viewed social corruption as a problem the Constitution was adequate to handle, the liberal-progressive tradition saw the Constitution as an obstacle to reform policy: the Constitution itself was corrupted as a science of politics and therefore was inadequate for the practical tasks of leadership in government. Taft described his understanding of this point as "progressive" in the broadest sense of the term: it recognized that changed circumstances required new legislative policies. Everyone, it would seem, was at least a little progressive. The difference between Taft and his critics, however, can be seen in the practical remedies that logically followed from the foundational arguments of the two sides. Their respective positions merit a more extended discussion.

The Initiative and Referendum and the Foundations of Constitutionalism

Because Taft could describe himself as a "progressive," at least in the sense that he regarded the American Founders as progressives in the broad sense of the term, he was forced to distinguish between two forms of progressivism. He described his own arguments as "another form of progressivism," designed to operate not only upon the collective conscience of Americans as citizens of a republic, but also upon the individual consciences of a leisure class of individuals who have, in their "mad chase for money," neglected their social responsibility "to lessen the burden and suffering of the poor and the oppressed under our present economic system, and render opportunities for self-betterment in society more nearly equal. There has arisen from the commercial spirit, a greater social consciousness."[36] The new form of liberal-progressivism, in Taft's analysis, has staked its policy proposals on increasing the functions of government in such a way that the notion of limited government with enumerated powers has become the enemy of reform and has argued that "The *laissez faire* school would have opposed such functions as paternalistic."[37] But Taft is not a *laissez faire* politician. What he does attempt to articulate, however vague it might seem at times, is the notion that limited government with enumerated powers has as one of its foundational principles a view of human nature that the Darwinian argument has eviscerated. There is, he says, "a line beyond which Government can not go with any good practical results in seeking to make men and society better."[38] The final problem, he suggests, is frankly "human nature," which he assumes has certain fixed properties that must be accounted for in any science of government. And human nature manifests itself in individuals first and in groups only in a secondary or abstract sense of sociological categories: society is man writ large and man is not society writ small. Taft does not deny that in a statistical sense it can easily be shown that different groups behave differently in their voting patterns: every practical politician recognizes as much whenever he or she runs for office. What Taft does deny is that group identity trumps the concept of citizenship rights that belong to all citizens equally and which will be eviscerated by proportional representation of groups.

It is important to emphasize here that it is not the motives of the new liberal-progressivism that are at issue in Taft's critique. The new school of political philosophers was not mistaken when it attacked the corruption of politics by corporate wealth and sought the alleviation of penury, and to change or qualify the right of property so as to more nearly equalize property conditions, represented a plan whose general purposes "all good men sympathize with."[39] But the practical means of dealing with these injustices is what troubles Taft: it is the push for more direct democracy within the context of a written constitution that is the crux of the problem. He stakes his opposition to more direct democracy on the proposition that there "is nothing to show that all legitimate governmental purposes sought by the so-called Progressives may not be promoted and brought about under the representative system."[40] It will be, he admits, slower to use the existing administrative process, but he does not accept that this amounts to a foundational criticism of the existing Constitution. On the contrary, it is one of the strengths of a written constitution with fixed political principles.

The political corruption, which both Taft and the "other form of progressivism" fully acknowledge, has its roots, he argues, not in the constitutional system, but in human nature. He writes, with considerable insight born of his experience in the White House, "it does not follow that politicians might not, if we had the other system, address themselves to its weaknesses and bring about a result quite as disheartening."[41] The real problem is not with the system but with people—with individual human nature. Politicians who promote corruption in whatever form will invariably find a way to use any system to their ends: "They might have to change their methods under the proposed changes to a more direct democracy, but if the people neglect their duties in politics the same manipulators could learn to turn the new system to their use quite as successfully as the old."[42] The prevention of corruption thus turns on how well citizenship is cultivated in any system of government. Any theory of how popular government *ought* to operate must be tested against what we may reasonably expect citizens to *do* following the proposed reforms. A criticism of the proposals for Initiative and Referendum, in Taft's argument, will then turn on whether these devices for a more direct democracy help or hinder the education of an enlightened citizenship. The citizenship and representational issues of "We the people" is not a rhetorical or abstract problem for Taft: it is *the* practical problem of popular government. Group rights will at best distort a constitutional system built on individual rights and the problem will manifest itself in the electoral process.

The referendum has long been known in "the political machinery of government," Taft wrote, and by itself does not pose a particular problem when it is part of a general election. Several states have experimented with the referendum, with mixed results, and Taft spends little time discussing their abstract pros and cons. When the issue is a municipal bond or the like, the issue is easily understood. But when the referendum stands alone in a special election, it is not likely to attract the vote of a majority of the electorate, and it is here the essence of the problem begins. The problem is as old as the tension between majority rule and minority rights that the Founders thought to be the bane of classical politics. "I have no hesitancy," he writes, "in saying that I think the requirement that the vote should be a majority of those voting at the election."[43] Otherwise, experience suggests, the issue is almost certain to be decided by a minority of voters. What is proposed as a democratic device winds up being a device that typically favors, in fact, a more intensely motivated minority. This problem is especially acute when the referendum proposes a change in the state constitution. In the process of too frequent voting on policy issues that are transformed by the referendum process into constitutional issues, state constitutions become less stable because they are subject to change on a regular basis: practical issues are transformed into constitutional issues to the impoverished political understanding of both. A fixed constitution "embodies the self-imposed restraint by the people upon those who act for them in passing laws or executing laws or policies."[44] When a constitution becomes a set of policies rather than a foundation for government, the effect on citizenship is to breed a loss of respect for the rule of law in those sections that have such laws imposed upon them by electoral majorities assembled elsewhere. What Taft doubts about such procedures is not their abstract constitutionality, but their harmful though indirect effects on citizenship.

When the referendum is combined with the initiative, the practical effect is not a more representative system, but one that is in fact less representative of the common good and less responsible to citizens in their collective equality before the law. "The new school of political philosophers proposes the referendum for far wider uses" than have traditionally been the case: the expansion of the traditional, limited referendum, into what was called the "compulsory referendum." The compulsory referendum as the new liberal-pro-gressives envisioned it was a complex device that requires an extraordinary number of legislative proposals be submitted annually to the people for a vote. "It is argued that in this way prompt action is secured in deference to popular will" and is less susceptible to corruption by powerful interests operating behind the legislative scenes. "However, the ease with which the so-called pure democracy can be turned to the advantage of the corruptionist has yet to be shown. His opportunity will be in the failure of the majority of the people to perform their heavier duty under the new sys-tem, and human nature has greatly changed if such opportunity will not be improved."[45]

More than this, he goes on to say, "the great advantage under the representative system is that it gives room for intelligent discussion and amendment, whereas under the initiative and referendum such opportunity for bettering the proposal and making it practical and useful is wholly wanting."[46] The manipulation of the pub-lic occurs when the drafters of the initiative and referendum frame the issue to be presented. It is a system designed to impose an impossible bur-den on the public to become knowledgeable on a range of issues that even seasoned administrators will have difficulty grappling with. "Representative government is said to be a failure because the people are not capable of selecting proper representatives. And yet the whole system of referendum and initiative rests upon the assumed intelligence and discretion of the people..."[47] It is, Taft thinks, a theory of democracy operating with conflicting and contradictory assumptions about how citizens behave or are likely to behave that will ultimately fail the test of popular government at the practical level.

The people, Taft writes, "are far better able to select candidates than they are to pass upon complicated questions of legislation.... Could any system be devised better adapted to the exaltation of cranks and the wearying of the electorate of their political duties than the giving the power to 5 per cent or even 8 percent of the voters to submit all the fads and nostrums that their active but impractical minds can devise, to be voted on in frequent elections?"[48] Further, "If the education of the people is necessary to make the new system work, does it not seem the course of common sense to retain the old system in which the lesson to be learned is so much simpler and so much more easily taught."[49] Requiring people to go to the polls as frequently as participatory democracy requires is likely to have the long-term effect of reducing the number of people who actually vote. As a practical matter, such a system will more likely be dominated by an active minority than the present system. Popular government is, Taft thinks, better protected by the Burkean representative "who acts on his own judgment as to what is best for his country and the people, even though this be contrary to the temporary popular notion or passion."[50] Somewhere and somehow, the Constitution must be part of the representative's constituency.

What most rouses Taft's constitutional ire, however, is the effect participatory democratic requirements have on constitutional principles. "The necessary result of the compulsory referendum following the initiative is to nullify and defeat the very advantages of the representative system which made it an improvement upon direct government."[51] Institutionally, the effect of the referendum is to diminish the power, and ultimately respect for, the legislative branch. A pure democracy, unfettered by a constitution such as the one bequeathed us by our Founders, is not one tethered to a conception of inalienable rights: no individual has any rights that a temporary voting majority may not alter or abolish. The Bill of Rights, he implies, will lose its meaning in a system that makes simple majority rule the foundational principle of popular government.

The Founders, he observes, "saw a possible tyranny in a majority in popular government quite as dangerous as the despotism of kings and they prepared a written constitution intended to preserve individual rights against its exercise."[52] Nothing less than the political character of a republican form of government is at issue and Taft has no doubt that such a system can be rationally defined and defended independent of the judiciary.[53] It is an argument for republican government with a strong dose of judicial restraint at its heart. It is, he thinks, an impatience with constitutional restraints that is the motivating factor behind the liberal-progressive argument.[54] And it is this impatience with constitutional restraints that reflects a latent hostility to popular government in any form if the *demos* should ever come to oppose the reformist agenda.

A More Perfect Union

After his critique of the initiative, referendum, and direct primary as practical proposals taken from the liberal-progressive arsenal, Taft returned to his original starting point with his discussion of another aspect of the Preamble to the Constitution captured in the phrase "In Order to Form a More Perfect Union." In many respects, it is his capstone argument, although it appears roughly in the middle of his collection of lectures: organizationally, the chapter might have been better placed at the end. Reading Taft with hindsight, and knowing of his later tenure as Chief Justice of the Supreme Court, students will tend, perhaps inescapably, to read his comments with an eye toward understanding his judicial philosophy. But they were not intended to be so read at the time because Taft did not yet entertain any serious belief that he could receive such an appointment: the results of the 1912 election where he received a scant 23 percent of the popular vote remains the most dismal showing of any incumbent presidential candidate since a popular vote for presidential electors began to be tallied in 1824.[55] Nevertheless, it is not a mistake to read the chapter with his subsequent judicial career in mind. As a foundation for later decisions on the bench, it is in fact an important chapter in Taft's constitutional interpretation, broadly defined.

The purpose of the Constitution, as James Madison defined it, is to secure public goods and private rights. Taft accepted this definition as axiomatic. It is the reason why he placed so much emphasis on republican citizenship that he thought participatory democracy would certainly weaken, if not destroy it altogether. Carrying out the general purpose of the Constitution is the meaning of the term "to form a more perfect union." The practical problem that emerges, therefore, centers on the question of how to institutionalize this purpose in a union that sometimes seems to be more disunited than united. The founders sought to institutionalize this purpose in a constitutional system in which no single institution could presume to have the final say on what the Constitution means on a disputed subject. The emerging liberal-progressive science of politics, however, destroyed the idea that constitutional interpretation had a fixed meaning. It was in the context of this quarrel over the very definition of a constitution that Taft engaged his adversaries on the meaning of a more perfect union. Without a more perfect union in a foundational sense, the purpose of republican government as Madison defined it could not be realized.

Taft well understood that the achievement of a more perfect union remains a work-in-progress: it was incomplete at the founding, incomplete in his day, and will probably remain incomplete as long as the Declaration of Independence and the Constitution remain the founding basis of American government. He begins his discussion of what the term means with a lengthy quote from Alexander Hamilton in *Federalist 15* on the necessity for the ratification of the Constitution on the grounds of national humiliation: the absence of a more perfect union, which requires a concentration of national power at the expense of the states, has imperiled both private rights and the public good. It is the longest quote Taft uses in his lectures and deserves more than passing notice, even by those thoroughly familiar with *The Federalist*. It is here that a close reading of this passage suggests that Taft's constitutional interpretation owes more to Hamilton than to Madison on broad matters of constitutional construction. Because this interpretation of Taft runs counter to the most commonly accepted view of Taft as a traditional conservative, this point needs some extended discussion.

First of all, when Taft quotes Madison from *The Federalist* he also carefully notes that Madison later, after the ratification of the Constitution, became the congressional ally of Jefferson. In making this alliance with Jefferson he profoundly changed his views on constitutional meaning.[56] Madison of *The Federalist* was, along with Alexander Hamilton and John Jay, a *nationalist* advocating a strong central government. It was the lack of a strong national government that was at the root of our national humiliation. "Mr. Jefferson and the strict constructionists who exalted the power of the states were the Republican party, which has now become the Democratic party."[57] Jefferson "finally carried Madison along with him in his strict constructionist views, although the latter had been one of the principle agents in framing the instrument and in bringing about its adoption." And Taft makes it clear in this context that he is a nationalist in the mold of Hamilton rather than a student of the later Madison on matters of broad constitutional construction. "The Federalist party, of which Washington may be said to have been the leader, and of which Hamilton was its most able exponent, was in control of the administration for three presidential terms..."[58] This practical adoption of the nationalist argument in *The Federalist*, combined with the appointment of John Marshall as Chief Justice of the Supreme Court, established the foundation for a national interpretation of the Constitution. "Had the views of Jefferson prevailed in the construction of the Constitution, the effect of that instrument would have been determined by the independent and varying judgments of the several States, and our nation would have been treated as a compact of several members, rather than as a sovereign nation."[59]

Despite the election of Jefferson in 1800, the nationalist argument of Hamilton and Washington triumphed, not in electoral politics, but in the opinions of Marshall from the Court. It is primarily the judiciary, therefore, that has best preserved the Founders' Constitution. On the one hand, it is not surprising that the future Chief Justice would side with Marshall on this point. Marshall is the "Great" Chief Justice and virtually all subsequent federal judicial appointments have paid him appropriate tribute. What is interesting here is to recall Taft's better known argument on executive power taken from *Our Chief Magistrate and His Powers*. It was Jefferson who argued for a strict construction of executive powers and Hamilton who argued for a broad interpretation, and Taft was no friend of Jefferson on this point.

The commonplace interpretation of Taft's reflections on executive power is to view it as more restrictive than either Theodore Roosevelt or Woodrow Wilson; but this is only partly true. Taft argued for a constitutional presidency in the tradition of Hamilton and not the open-ended interpretation of executive powers implied in Roosevelt's "stewardship theory." Taft explicitly argued that war and foreign affairs carried a constitutional logic for executive supremacy that a Jeffersonian construction did not support. Taft did not view executive power as restrictive in times of war and he certainly did not accept a notion of legislative supremacy as somehow rooted in the founding principles of *The Federalist*. He fully approved of the entire range of Lincoln's use of war and foreign affairs powers during the Civil War. As a general principle, "it is the present text of the fundamental law that determines who shall exercise the powers which it confers, and I do not understand why the function that the Senate performs is any more important or any more sacred than that of the Executive..."[60] The complexities of war "seem to differ with the character of the nation whose relations with the United States are affected."[61] This does not render the Constitution null—the President could not declare war, for example, but it does trigger extraordinary executive powers under the "Commander-in-Chief" clause that Taft saw exercised by every wartime president.

He noted, accurately and importantly, that each war produces novelties that require presidential action and that there "was nothing new or startling in the principle of his temporary enlargement of his executive functions."[62] The point here is not to split hairs over executive powers *per se*, but to draw our attention to the foundational basis for Taft's reasoning about constitutional construction that can be traced to his views in *Popular Government*. As one scholar has pointed out, "Underlying the negative image of law that both Roosevelt and

Wilson invoked was the unspoken assumption
that the act of construing the Constitution (or any
law) is antithetical to political decision making."[63]
What made Taft's arguments different from either
those of Roosevelt or Wilson was not a notion of
legislative dominance of the executive in these
matters. Rather, it is the foundational basis for
constitutional construction that separates them.
Constitutional reasoning about war and foreign
affairs powers is not necessarily antithetical to
practical political decision-making. The liberal-
progressive tradition that Taft opposed did not
believe the Founders' Constitution was adequate
for a modern nation: serious political decision-
making took place outside constitutional restrictions. Taft's reasoning was more along the lines of
Hamilton in his "Pacificus" essays contra Madison
1793-1794, and certainly did not reflect a narrow
"Whig" reading of the Constitution.[64]

What gives more than a touch or irony to Taft's
constitutional construction at this point is to set
it alongside the defining thesis of Herbert Croly:
that the aim of the liberal-progressive movement
was to wed Hamiltonian ends of government to
Jeffersonian means.[65] Leaving aside the theoretical incoherence of this popular but dubious thesis,
Croly's statement summed-up the liberal-progressive argument over political means in a nutshell:

they saw themselves as democrats prepared to use the engine of the national government in order to achieve a particular policy agenda. They took it for granted that this would require an abandonment of the Founders' Constitution and the science of politics that lay behind it. But war and foreign affairs powers are at the crossroads of the Founders' theory and practice of republican government. If a republican theory of popular government cannot resolve this most vexing issue, republican political science will also contain the seeds of its own destruction. War is, in many respects, the acid test of popular government.

What liberal-progressives such as Croly and Wilson took to be a rupture of ends and means in the founding principles of the regime, Taft saw as a complementary relationship: the foundational principles of the Constitution were sufficient to accommodate both change and stability. But when the emphasis was placed on change without a foundation, stability was jeopardized. Taft was far more of a Hamiltonian in both ends and means in the sense that he took a more expansive view of the constitutional grants of power than did the liberal-progressives. Under the Marshall Court, he wrote, "The Court refused to limit the implication of powers to those who were indispensable to the exercise of the express powers, but held that any method of carrying out the express powers which was reasonable and proper, was in the discretion of Congress."[66]

Taft held to the opinion that, due to a series of "fortuitous circumstances," constitutional construction by the Supreme Court naturally tended to uphold national power when it conflicted with state power. Whatever force the Jeffersonian theory of government had in practice, the judicial power tended to be Federalist and provided a powerful counterweight to arguments for legislative supremacy and for states' rights broadly defined. The Constitution does not need to be amended or interpreted in radically new ways for it to function as the Founders intended. "Circumstances in the growth of the country have served greatly to increase the volume of federal power. This has not come from a new construction of the Constitution, but it has come from the fact that the federal power has been enlarged by the expansion of the always conceded subjects of national activities."[67] He goes on to note, "This great expansion of Federal activities has been almost within the recollection, and by the agency, of living men; but it has not changed the *form* [emphasis mine] of our government..."[68] The Constitutional autonomy of the states is built into the original constitutional design, and national supremacy on matters that

require national policy is not jeopardized by ad-
herence to the Founders' science of republican
government. It is only when the new political
philosophers start with a new set of foundational
assumptions that the Constitution begins to appear inadequate to the task of providing a popular
form of government. A pure form of democracy,
Taft observes, echoing Madison in *Federalist 10*,
is not possible in a nation as large as the United
States. It is an error of the first order to believe
that the principles associated with participatory democracy can be followed in a republican
constitution without doing grievous harm to the
polity.

Popular Government *in an Era of Progressivism*

When *Popular Government* was published by
Yale in 1913 it was initially limited to 2,000 copies: a second edition was limited to 1,000 copies.
Among academics, it appears to have attracted
little notice, unlike *Our Chief Magistrate and
His Powers*, which did attract attention. Perhaps
its appearance following Taft's dismal showing
in the 1912 election had something to do with
it. But more important has been the dominance
of the liberal-progressive tradition of academic

scholarship that has dominated the academy since the days of Roosevelt and Wilson. The emerging scholars in this tradition dismissed Taft as a "re-actionary" and never seriously tried to understand his constitutional construction, much less the foundational arguments that supported it: they were too critical of the Founders at every level of analysis to see anything in Taft that might be use-ful or important in building up a body of practical knowledge in the administration of public affairs. Taft sensed this when he wrote, "Those of us who are thus unjustly classed must be content to be so until vindicated by the event. But we must fight for our principles and maintain them without fear, because unless we do so, as I verily believe, our form of representative democracy will be destroyed and its power to aid and maintain the happiness of the individual will cease."[69]

Whether Taft was too pessimistic or not on this score may depend in part on the time frame we might have in mind for the ultimate demise of the Republic—a few dozen years or a few dozen centu-ries. His point invites two plausible responses: (1) that the liberal-progressive science Taft inveighed against so strongly was not really as radical as ei-ther Taft or his adversaries said it was, or (2) that the liberal-progressive political science of Wilson and others has met sufficient resistance at various levels that whatever its influence it has never completely taken hold in American politics. I am more inclined toward the latter view and it is for this reason that Taft holds a special place in these debates: he is the most visible critic of liberal-progressivism during that period in American history when the arguments of Wilson and others were in their infancy. In this sense, Taft's perspective remains unique. It is typically in the foundation of such arguments that their principles are most visible—when nothing can be taken for granted, whether it is *The Federalist* or Wilson.

No doubt persons of wide political descriptions will find much to disagree with regarding many of the specific reforms Taft supported or opposed. But if we only focus on policy we will miss the heart of Taft's argument. Taft may have been in error on any number of details, but such details do not get at the question of what makes Taft worth reading a century after he left office. What makes him worth reading depends upon how we view the consequences of the dueling arguments in American political science that originated during the Progressive Era and have shaped American political discourse ever since. How did the arguments over constitutional meaning affect both our collective self-understanding of the nature of the American regime and the practice of American politics? I use the term "meaning" here rather than "construction" or "interpretation" because meaning seems to me broader. Taft points us in the direction of thinking about meaning in the Founders' sense of the term.

Much of contemporary political thought and constitutional interpretation pits the Founders' Constitution against the "living constitution" school of Wilson and others. But such terms as "living constitution," "original intent," or "original meaning," useful as they might be in specific circumstances, do not quite touch on what is involved. Supreme Court Justice Antonin Scalia has argued that the living constitution school of jurisprudence has trivialized the Constitution by making constitutional decisions little more than a series of ordinary common law decisions.[70] And indeed it must be said that Taft did not fully appreciate all of the consequences of those arguments with which he battled, however sound his instincts may have been: it would never have occurred to him that constitutional decisions by the Supreme Court could ever be described as akin to "common law decisions." But there is a precedent for what he was getting at and we may catch a glimpse of it by briefly turning to Tocqueville for some light on the subject.

Tocqueville observed that since the argument for modern democracy was new he could find no example from the past that would shed light on what he was trying to describe: he would have to content himself with merely describing it. His concern was for "democratic tyranny" that he thought would be quite unlike any previous experience with political tyranny. Since Tocqueville's time the democratic phenomenon and the problem of democratic tyranny that so animated him have taken several turns; one road has been toward the further development of freedom in a liberal democracy in the mold of the American Revolution and the other the road followed from the mold of the French Revolution that led to precisely the sort of tyranny Tocqueville had in mind.[71] Leo Strauss identified the change associated with the latter as built on the abandonment of natural law by academic scholarship that had the effect of validating the idea of historicism—the notion that everything, including moral principles, is relative. It was this Hegelian historicism, he thought, that had ruined German philosophy and through its value relativism had intellectually helped to pave the way for Fascism.[72] Neither Strauss nor any other serious scholars have ever thought of American liberal-progressivism as a harbinger of Fascism. But the political science of liberal-progressivism, like all theories of politics, carries within itself the intellectual seeds of its own form of tyranny: a value relativism born of the Darwinian model of democratic evolution. The likelihood that these seeds may bear their unwanted fruit will be dramatically increased if the foundational arguments of popular government are lost or forgotten. Tocqueville thought such a tyranny would be unlike any we have ever experienced: it would degrade men rather than torment them. Of democratic people Tocqueville wrote, "I do not fear that in their chiefs they will find tyrants, but rather schoolmasters."[73]

Tocqueville laid great stress on the manners, the customs, and the internalized moral character of Americans to prevent the sort of tyranny he had in mind and the sort that overwhelmed Europe in the twentieth century. In America, for example, democracy and religion mutually supported each other; in Europe they went their separate ways. The American experiment resulted in freedom and that part of the European experiment that followed a secularized theory of progress resulted in tyranny. Whatever may be true of academic opinion as a whole, some very sober students of American political development have come to wonder if Tocqueville's fears about democratic tyranny might be closer at the outset of the twenty-first century than at any time since Tocqueville wrote.[74] Culture can change, and the culture of constitutional construction has changed dramatically since Taft wrote.

Taft could write that a series of fortuitous circumstances kept the Supreme Court in the hands of jurists who followed Marshall and *The Federalist* understanding of republican government. But at the beginning of the twenty-first century it is doubtful that any constitutional scholar would make such an observation as the terms "democrat" and "republican" have become virtually synonymous, save for a few scholars who work the field. And with the loss of these distinctions, the foundations of free government and the dangers of democratic tyranny have both been drained of their original meanings. The Darwinian worldview, with its radically secularized view of progress, has no doubt played a role in these changes. And it is no doubt also true that all of the changes may not be what Wilson intended. But we also know that ideas often have unintended consequences. The implicit moral and political relativism of Wilson's constitutionalism left no principled foundation from which to defend free government or to recognize tyranny.

Finally, we return to a rereading of Taft's quarrels with Roosevelt, Wilson, and the liberal-progressive tradition because those quarrels have not yet completely played themselves out, either in the academic or in the political arena of elective politics: perhaps they never will, with each side experiencing temporary ups and downs. And it may be a truism in defending free government that sometimes it is defended by the very same persons who have cut themselves off from the foundational arguments of freedom embodied in *The Federalist*. Neither Roosevelt nor Wilson should be viewed as enemies of free government by any serious student of American political thought: nor should Taft be so regarded by students who have learned their constitutional construction from Wilson. The quarrels remain important for any understanding of the problems that perpetually confront the American experiment in popular government because in the twenty-first century we have a longer perspective on these arguments and their subsequent consequences than did either Taft or Wilson.

We may compare the significance of these differences between political factions by briefly recalling James Madison's understanding of factions and what to do about them: he wrote, "As long as the reason of man continues fallible, and he is at liberty to exercise it, different opinions will be formed.... The latent causes of faction are thus sown in the nature of man; and we see them every where brought into different degrees of activity, according to the different circumstances of civil society" (*Fed. 10*). But Madison could afford to take what may seem to us a relatively benign view of policy quarrels between various factions within the American polity because, whatever the policy differences among them, he could also assume the foundational reality of "self evident Truths" as a basis for argument. Any serious student of the American experiment in popular government will be compelled to observe here that by the time Taft retired from the White House to defend the founders' Constitution, such Madisonian assumptions could no longer be taken for granted. And rereading Taft a century after he penned his critique of the liberal-progressive arguments of Roosevelt and Wilson, the notion of constitutional government built on "self-evident Truths" will perhaps seem even quainter among some than it did then.

Sidney A. Pearson, Jr.
Radford University

Notes

1. I would like to thank my friends Matthew Franck and Anne Pierce for patiently reading an earlier version of the manuscript and making numerous helpful suggestions which have materially improved its final form. They are, of course, wholly innocent of any responsibility for the final version can only take whatever solace they may find in knowing that it is at least better than it would otherwise have been.

2. One interesting exception to this is David K. Nichols, *The Myth of the Modern Presidency*. (University Park, Pennsylvania: The Pennsylvania State University Press, 1994). Nichols takes the position that the Constitution is so open-ended in terms of executive power that, in effect, the Roosevelt-Taft argument is an argument not over constitutional interpretation, but personal, and, therefore, idiosyncratic ideas of how executive power ought to be used. It is a unique argument not shared by most other students of the presidency who think the quarrel between Taft and Roosevelt is, after all, about something constitutional.

3. Taft has never fared well among scholarly attempts to rank presidents in order of "greatness" and it seems unlikely that he ever will. But it should be noted that lawyers have generally given him higher marks than historians. See the discussion of ranking presidents in James Taranto and Leonard Leo (Eds.), *Presidential Leadership: Rating the Best and the Worst in the White House*. (New York: Free Press, 2004), esp. the fine discussion on methodology and characteristics of ranking surveys, pp. 249-266.

4. Theodore Roosevelt, *An Autobiography*. New York: Charles Scribner's Sons, 1913. P. 357.

5. *The Collected Works of William Howard Taft*. David W. Burton, General Editor. Vol. VI. (Athens, Ohio: Ohio University Press, 2003). Edited with Commentary by W. Carey McWilliams and Frank X. Gerrity, p. 3.

6. William Howard Taft, *Our Chief Magistrate and His Powers*. (New York: Columbia University Press, 1916), pp. 139-140. Hereafter cited as *CM*.

7. Typical are the remarks in Louis W. Koenig, *The Chief Executive*. Second Edition. (New York: Harcourt, Brace & World, 1968), p. 10. The term "Whig" theory of government in the progressive tradition is borrowed directly from Woodrow Wilson's *Constitutional Government in the United States*. (New York: Columbia University Press, 1908; New Brunswick, NJ: Transaction Publishers, 2002), esp. Chapter III, "The President of the United States," pp. 54-81.Taft's argument is also frequently described as a "strict construction" interpretation of Article II of the Constitution, as for example Michael A. Genovese, *The Power of the American Presidency 1789-2000*. (New York: Oxford University Press, 2001), p. 116. On the Progressive critique in general on this point, see

Raymond Tatlovich and Thomas S. Engeman, *The Presidency and Political Science. Two Hundred Years of Constitutional Debate.* (Baltimore: The Johns Hopkins University Press, 2003), pp. 67-88.

8. Edward S. Corwin, *The President. Office and Powers 1787-1957. History and Analysis of Practice and Opinion.* Fourth Revised Edition. (New York: New York University Press, 1957), p. 153-154.

9. Wilson, *Constitutional Government*, p. 55.

10. Some might argue that the impact of Hegelian historicism was, in fact reasonably well understood even at the time. See Jurgen Herbst, *The German Historical School in American Scholarship. A Study in the Transfer of Culture.* (Ithaca, New York: Cornell University Press, 1965). David M. Ricci, *The Tragedy of Political Science. Politics, Scholarship, and Democracy.* (New Haven: Yale University Press, 1984).

11. See Roger M. Barrus, John H. Eastby, Joseph H. Lane, Jr., David E. Marion and James F. Pontuso, *The Deconstitutionalization of America. The Forgotten Frailties of Democratic Rule.* (Lanham, MD: Lexington Books, 2004).

12. The best work on the importance of foundational concepts in political science is James W. Ceaser, *Nature and History in American Political Development. A Debate.* (Cambridge, MA: Harvard University Press, 2006). See especially Ceaser's response to his critics, pp. 171-197.

13. McWilliams, *Op. Cit.*, p. 5.

14. Stephen Skowronek, *The Politics Presidents Make. Leadership from John Adams to George Bush.* (Cambridge, MA: Harvard University Press, 1993), pp. 243-259.

15. William Howard Taft, *Popular Government. Its Essence, Its Permanence and Its Perils.* (New Haven: Yale University Press, 1913), p. 16. Hereafter cited as *PG*.

16. It should be noted, appropriately as a footnote at this point, that Yale Law School had converted to the "case-law" method of legal education shortly before Taft arrived to deliver his lectures. Taft had learned law using what was known as the "textbook method." The tendency of the case-law method of legal teaching is to make all law look like judge-made law: if you want to know the meaning of a law, look to see what judges have said about it. This approach suffices for ordinary common law, but can prove fatal for Constitutional law because it tends to make it appear that the Constitu-

tion is simply what the judge says it is: absent a judicial interpretation, it appears that the Constitution has no independent meaning that can be rationally discerned. The textbook method, whatever its faults, did at least help to teach students that Constitutional interpretation was, at its foundation, independent of strictly judicial interpretation. On the reduction of modern Constitutional law to common law, see Antonin Scalia, *A Matter of Interpretation. Federal Courts and the Law*. (Princeton: Princeton University Press, 1997).

17. *PG*, p. 8.
18. *Ibid.*, p. 15.
19. *Ibid.*, p. 9.
20. *Ibid.*, p. vii.
21. This point is carefully explored in Anthony A. Peacock, *Deconstructing the Republic. Voting Rights, the Supreme Court, and the Founders' Republicanism Reconsidered*. (Washington, DC: American Enterprise Institute Press, 2008).
22. *PG.*, p. 2.
23. *Ibid.*, p. 2.
24. *Ibid.*, p. 11.
25. *Ibid.*, pp. 18-19.
26. *Ibid.*, p. 21.
27. *Ibid.*, p. 34-25.
28. *Ibid.*, p. 26.
29. *Ibid.*, p. 28.
30. Frank J. Goodnow, *Politics and Admninistration. A Study in Government*. (New York: The Macmillan Company, 1900), p. 199.
31. See Sidney A. Pearson, Jr., Transaction Introduction: "E. E. Schattschneider and the Quarrel Over Parties in American Democracy," in E. E. Schattschneider, *Party Government* (New Brunswick, NJ: Transaction Publishers, 2004/New York: Farr and Reinehart, 1941).
32. James W. Ceaser, *Presidential Selection. Theory and Development*. (Princeton: Princeton University Press, 1979).
33. *PG*, pp. 29-30.
34. *Ibid.*, p. 33.
35. *Ibid.*, pp. 33-34.
36. *Ibid.*, pp. 34-35.
37. *Ibid.*, p. 35.
38. *Ibid.*, p. 35.

39. *Ibid.*, p. 37.
40. *Ibid.*, pp. 37-38.
41. *Ibid.*, p. 38.
42. *Ibid.*, p. 40.
43. *Ibid.*, p. 43.
44. *Ibid.*, 9. 44.
45. *Ibid.*, pp. 48, 50.
46. *Ibid.*, p. 51.
47. *Ibid.*, pp. 51-52. A collection of contemporary essays on the subject can be found in William Bennett Munro (Ed.), *The Initiative Referendum and Recall.* (New York: D. Appleton and Company, 1913). See also the interesting letter by Woodrow Wilson to Prof. R. H. Dabney, "On the Initiative, Referendum and Recall," in Woodrow Wilson, *The Public Papers of Woodrow Wilson. College and State.* Edited by Ray Stannard Baker and William E. Dodd. Vol. II. (New York: Harper & Brothers Publishers, 1925), pp. 323-324. The letter was printed in *Richmond Times Dispatch*, December 26, 1911. It is unlikely that Taft read Wilson's letter, but he did not exaggerate the argument.
48. *PG*, p. 54.
49. *Ibid.*, p. 59.
50. *Ibid.*, p. 60.
51. *Ibid.*, p. 64.
52. *Ibid.*, p. 67.
53. *Ibid.*, 78.
54. *Ibid.*, p. 94.
55. The 1912 presidential election was essentially a four-way electoral contest. Woodrow Wilson (Democrat), won with 41.8% of the vote; Theodore Roosevelt (Progressive), received 27.2%; William Howard Taft (Republican), 23.2%; Eugene V. Debs (Socialist) received 6%. Other candidates received about 1.6% of the total vote cast.
56. Although Taft does not cite it, this change is perhaps nowhere more evident than in Madison's exchange with Hamilton over executive power in the *Pacificus-Helvidius* debates. It is instructive to compare and contrast Madison's arguments in these later debates with his earlier argument in *The Federalist*, especially *Fed. 41*, where he seems to be more in agreement with a Hamiltonian understanding of executive war and foreign affairs powers.
57. *PG.*, p. 127.

58. *Ibid.*, p. 130.
59. *Ibid.*, pp. 131-132.
60. *CM*, p. 106.
61. *Ibid.*, p. 95.
62. *Ibid.*, p. 99.
63. H. Jefferson Powell, "Editor's Introduction: The Context of Taft's Lectures," in William Howard Taft, *Our Chief Magistrate and His Powers.* (Durham, North Carolina: Carolina Academic Press, 2002), p. xxxiii. This edition is to be recommended because of the most insightful essay by Powell. It is a model for an introductory essay interpreting an important work such as the one by Taft. I am very much influenced by Powell's interpretation of Taft's thought. See also Powell's *The President's Authority Over Foreign Affairs. An Essay in Constitutional Interpretation.* (Durham, North Carolina: Carolina Academic Press, 2002). Powell's interpretation of war and foreign affairs powers of the President seems to follow, appropriately updated, Taft's understanding of constitutional construction in this vital area.
64. In this context, see Morton J. Frisch, "The Significance of the Pacificus-Helvidius Debates: Toward the Completion of the American Founding," in Morton J. Frisch, (Ed.), *The Pacificus-Helvidius Debates of 1793-1794.* (Indianapolis, Indiana: The Liberty Fund, 2007).
65. Herbert Croly, *The Promise of American Life.* (New York: The Macmillan Company, 1909/Cambridge, Massachusetts: Harvard University Press, 1965), pp. 213-214.
66. *PG*, p. 133.
67. *Ibid.*, p. 138.
68. *Ibid.*, p. 144.
69. *Ibid.*, p. 37.
70. Scalia, *Matter of Interpretation. Op. Cit.*
71. The term is borrowed from J. L. Talmon, *The Origins of Totalitarian Democracy.* (New York: Frederick A. Praeger Publishers, 1960).
72. Leo Strauss, *Natural Right in History.* (Chicago: The University of Chicago Press, 1953).
73. Alexis de Tocqueville, *Democracy in America.* Translated, Edited, and with an Introduction by Harvey C. Mansfield and Delba Winthrop. (Chicago: University of Chicago Press, 2000), p. 662.

74. This point has been advanced with considerable insight in Hugh Heclo, *Christianity and American Democracy*. (Cambridge, MA: Harvard University Press, 2007). Heclo's thesis is advanced, appropriately enough, as the second of the Alexis de Tocqueville Lectures on American Politics sponsored by Harvard University.

INTRODUCTION

I came to Yale to assume my duties as Kent Professor of Law near the end of the school year, when it was not practical to add my courses of constitutional law to the then curriculum. It was suggested, therefore, that during the spring term, I prepare and deliver a course of lectures on some questions of modern government. This I did, making my text the preamble of the Constitution of the United States. In explaining the meaning of "We, the people," used to describe the source of political power, I thought it relevant and important to discuss the proposed changes from our republican form of government to a more direct, democratic government, and this led me to consider the initiative, the referendum and the recall, and also the direct primary, which, while not necessarily involved with the other issues, properly suggested itself for consideration with them.

Under the clause of the preamble "to form a more perfect union," I considered very briefly the historical issue between those who favored the broad construction of the Federal powers under the Constitution, and those who took the States' rights view.

Under the clause, "to establish justice," I discussed the subject of recall of judges and the recall of judicial decisions.

Under the phrase "to provide for the common defense," I considered the question of war and peace, under the Constitution, the army and the navy and their present needs, and the question of settlement of international controversies through diplomatic negotiation and by arbitration.

At the meeting of the American Bar Association, at Montreal, in September last, I read two addresses, one on "The Selection and Tenure of Judges," and the other on "The Social Importance of Proper Standards for Admission to the Bar." In the latter, I dealt with "judge-made" law. These addresses were closely related to the subjects treated of in my lecture on the establishment of justice under the Federal Constitution, and seemed an appropriate supplement. The Yale University lectures were eight in number, and, with the addresses at the American Bar Association, make the ten chapters which follow.

Since I have prepared this book for the press, the valuable and interesting volume of President Lowell of Harvard, on "Public Opinion and Popular Government" in the American Citizen Series, has been issued, in which he discusses in a most satisfactory way the actual operation of the initiative, the referendum and the recall, and gives a valuable résumé of the result of the use of these processes of direct government in Switzerland and in the states where they have been adopted.

I have not had the time to support the views that I have stated by such citations from official sources, but I am glad to be advised that the specific instances of record he gives are in general accord with my conclusions.

I am very hopeful that while this movement for more direct government now seems to be spreading, actual experience under it in the states that have tried it longest is convincing the members of the various electorates who have seen it work that it is not a panacea, and that it is developing evils of its own that will require at least a partial retracing of their steps.

WM. H. TAFT.

I

The Meaning of "We, the People of the United States," in the Preamble of the Constitution

It is my aim to discuss the subject of popular government under the Federal Constitution, and certain current issues as to the wisdom and soundness of the principles upon which its provisions are based.

If I had attempted the treatment of this subject ten years ago, my task would have been easier than it is to-day, for in the last decade a school of political thinkers has arisen by whom the wisdom and equity of our fundamental law have been seriously questioned and the justice of the common law, inherited from England and modified by judicial decision and statute, is attacked as not squaring with the proper civic and social and economic ideals of to-day.

It is difficult, therefore, to enter upon this discussion without taking up political, sociological and economic questions. As one reads the slashing criticism of everything which he accepted without argument when a student of constitutional history and governmental law twenty years ago, he finds himself suffering dizzy sensations for want of stable ground upon which to stand. Not only are the views of those who made the Constitution said to be unsound and outworn, but these Fathers of the Republic are themselves severely arraigned because of their alleged class feeling as land owners and creditors. We have been accustomed to muckraking in the case of living public men, but it is novel to impeach our institutions which have stood the test of more than a century by similar methods with reference to their founders, now long dead.

I can not think that this school of political philosophy will ultimately triumph. That some of its views may contain elements of truth and useful principle, requiring some changes and amendments in our fundamental law, may well be; but that it can justify and secure a radical change in the structure of our Government, and do away with its character as a Republic, based on the principles of popular representation, I can not believe.

The doctrines of the new school have been put into practice in a number of the States, and have acquired a vogue that is likely to extend their application. But one of the saving qualities of the

American people is their ability to make mistakes, to take a wrong course, and then to retrace it when the results and facts show them the truth. They frequently have to incur a very considerable cost in learning these lessons, but, as a people, they are quick to appreciate them, and do not seem to have pride of opinion that will keep them from a change, even in the short period of a presidential term. Therefore, while we may expect this "remedy of infusing more democracy in our existing democracy" to continue for a time, we have reason to hope that its obvious inconveniences, the appearance of new evils in its use and the probable return in possibly different forms of the old grievances for which these changes are now regarded as a sovereign cure, will ultimately convince the people that the difficulty in the operation of our present machinery has not been in its lack of adaptability to our needs, but it has been due to the failure of a majority of the people to discharge their duty as responsible members of a political community. Upon those of us, therefore, who appear to be in the minority in opposing these new governmental devices, the duty is plain of pointing out their defects and awaiting the event to demonstrate the truth of what we say. I would not say that one kind of political machinery is not better than another for securing good government and the expression of sober popular will, but I would say that, generally speaking, between the two systems, if the real reason why one does not work is the failure of the people to discharge their duty thereunder, a new system is not likely to work any better, when if properly discharged, the duty of the people is more onerous than before.

In examining the Constitution, the first clause that one reads is the preamble. The preamble is a general declaration of the Convention as to the purposes of the Constitution. The preamble has been much used in argument in the Supreme Court to aid the construction of the Constitution. The title of an act—and I presume the preamble of the Constitution comes within such a description—can hardly be used to change the actual language used in the body of the instrument which is to control. Still it throws light upon the document. It will be useful to follow its phrases as a general plan for my discussion of popular government in the United States, its advantages, its purpose, its essence, its safeguards and its perils.

The preamble is as follows:

"We, the people of the United States, in order to form a more perfect union, establish justice, insure domestic tranquillity, provide for the common defence, promote the general welfare, and secure the blessings of liberty to ourselves and our posterity, do ordain and establish this Constitution for the United States of America."

I ask your consideration, therefore, of the first phrase, "We, the people of the United States."

These words became very important in the controversy that arose as to the construction of the Constitution soon after its adoption, and which continued until the end of the Civil War. The theory of those who construed the Constitution so as to restrict and minimize, as far as possible, the powers conferred upon the National Government, contended that the Constitution was in effect not much more than a mere compact between the several sovereign States, who retained their independence and sovereignty as to everything except that which was expressly or by inevitable implication conferred upon the central government.

The other view was that taken by those who wished to enlarge the national power by every reasonable and useful implication from the powers expressly conferred in the Constitution. The strict constructionists, like Mr. Jefferson and Mr. Calhoun, contended that the use of the words, "We, the people of the United States," meant that the peoples of the several States, as different state units, were entering into a compact with each other to part with some of their faculties to form a central government in order to accomplish the purposes stated in the preamble. On the other hand, Chief Justice Marshall and the Supreme Court of the United States, in many decided cases, held that the words indicated that the body of the whole people of the United States, assembled, it is true, in the different States, because they could not assemble together, but acting as a whole people, were forming a new government of their own by ordaining and establishing the Constitution, and were to be recognized in the adoption of this fundamental instrument as the original source of the newly created Federal powers. This view made the whole people a possible depositary of some of the powers not granted to the National Government, and prevented the inference that the States were necessarily the depositary of all such reserved powers.

It is noteworthy, as a matter of history, that when President Jefferson was in the Presidency, and felt called upon to fill a vacancy in the Supreme Court, he appointed Mr. Joseph Story, of Massachusetts, a member of the then Republican party, evidently with the expectation that his view of the Constitution would be opposed to that of Chief Justice Marshall. The personality and the great ability of the illustrious Chief

Justice, however, exercised great influence over the brilliant young Justice, appointed at thirty-two, and when he came to pronounce his first great constitutional judgment as the organ of the Supreme Court, in the case of Martin vs. Hunter's lessee, in 1816, 1st Wheaton, 324, he announced the view of the Court that the Constitution of the United States was ordained and established, not by the States in their sovereign capacities, respectively represented by the different peoples thereof, but by the people as a body of the United States as a whole, and that this was the meaning of the preamble. This was confirmed by other judgments of that Court, notably by Chief Justice Marshall in the great cases of McCulloch vs. Maryland, 4th Wheaton, 316, and Osborn vs. the Bank, 9th Wheaton, 738. All these cases gave the Constitution liberal construction in favor of the powers of the National Government, and as the views expressed were opposed to those of Mr. Jefferson and the then Republicans, Mr. Justice Story was attacked as a renegade of the party. His views and those of his colleagues were regarded as most heretical by Mr. Calhoun and by his disciples. It is not very important now, except from an historical standpoint, to review the distinctions that were made before the Civil War in this all-absorbing issue, because the view taken by the broad constructionists was vindicated and made permanently to prevail by the arbitrament of the sword, and the theory of the Federal Constitution as a compact between sovereign States has as fully disappeared as the constitution of the Southern Confederacy itself.

The use of the words, "We, the people," was an indication on the part of the makers of the Constitution that they thought they were establishing a popular government, because a popular government may properly be defined to be a government established and maintained by the authority of the people. We are in favor of popular government because we believe that the fact that the people govern themselves will make them constant in its support and will secure obedience to the laws their representatives make and the executive they elect. This is likely to make the government strong and its protection of its individual citizens effective.

Moreover, experience sustains the view that every class of citizens in a community—and by a class I mean those who are similarly situated and conditioned—is more certain to look well after its own real interests than any other class, however altruistic. Hence a government in which every class has a voice, that is, a popular government, is more certain to do justice to each class and make proper provision for its welfare. This has only one exception, and that is, where a class has not intelligence enough to understand its own interest or rights.

Now popular government is not an end. It is a means of enabling people to live together in communities, municipal, state and national, and under these conditions to secure to each individual and each class of individuals the greatest measure of happiness. It was to aid this ultimate purpose that our Constitution was adopted. It was not thought by the people who made and ratified it that the majority could always be trusted certainly to accord to the individual just and equitable treatment in his pursuit of happiness. The people, themselves, imposed the restraints upon their own political action contained in the Constitution, the chief of which were the guaranties of individual rights. The security of these rights and all our civil institutions are nothing but means for the promotion of the happiness of the individual and his progress and are to be so regarded.

I know that the so-called individualistic theory of rights and duties has been attacked as not broad enough and that pressure is now being exerted to introduce into practical jurisprudence the view that class or collectivist rights and obligations should be more clearly recognized and enforced at the expense of the present so-called

rights of the individual. I am not now considering this issue and am not intimating any opinion
on it. Whatever the proper view, whether we
should continue to preserve individualism intact,
or qualify it by collectivist amendment, the ultimate purpose of government and its limitations
must be conceded to be the same, the promotion
of the happiness of the average individual and his
progress, whether this be effected by exalting individual independence, or by giving more power to
society to secure greater happiness to a greater
number of individuals.

The effect of these restraints to secure justice
and right for the individual reacts in favor of the
strength and permanence of the government of
the people. The tyranny and injustice of a
majority would be certain in the end to stir those
individuals suffering it to revolt, and would lead
to a change in the form of government, perhaps
to a one-man control. Such was the fate of
Greece, of Rome, and of France. The rule of the
people which is just and equal to all should endure
forever. Of course this permanence reciprocally
promotes individual happiness.

If, then, the distinction between what is the end
of government and what are the means by which
that government is to be bettered and may more
nearly reach its end, is kept clearly in mind, we

shall eliminate from the difficulties of political discussion a good many fetishes that now lie in wait for the unsophisticated reformer.

The preamble of the Constitution uses the phrase "We, the people of the United States," and I have been attempting to state the advantages of a popular government and its purpose. What is its essence? What is meant by "We, the people"? What is meant by "popular government"? If these terms are to be construed as referring to a government by all the people, then there never has been, and there never will be, and there never can be, a truly popular government, because it is impossible that all the people, i.e., all the individuals in the community, municipal, state or national, should have either the capacity or the opportunity to take actual part in its government. This is a fact the importance of which has not always been fully recognized.

Who were "the people" in the days when this Constitution was adopted? They were not the whole 4,000,000 of those who lived in the thirteen colonies. At least that 4,000,000 did not select the members of the Constitutional Convention. The members of that Convention were selected in popular colonial conventions in some colonies and by the legislatures of other colonies, and in the latter some of the delegates were confirmed by popular conventions. Now who voted to select the delegates for those conventions or legislatures? They were the qualified electorate of each colony, or at least a majority of the members of the electorate who took the trouble to vote. We know from the colonial laws who were qualified to vote, and we have an estimate made by those who have investigated it as to the ratio of that part to the total population.

Generally in the thirteen colonies, those who could vote were limited to men who owned a certain amount of property or paid a certain amount of taxes, and in some of the States they were required to be believers in the Protestant Christian religion.

In New Hampshire the voter had to be a Protestant and a tax-payer. In Massachusetts he had to be possessed of an income from a freehold estate of £3 a year, or to own a personal estate worth £60. In Connecticut he was obliged to have an annual income of $7 from a freehold estate, or real estate rated on the tax list as worth $134. In New York he was required to have a freehold estate of £30, or a house rent of 40s. In New Jersey any person, male or female, black or white, native or alien, was permitted to vote, if only he or she owned real estate worth £50. In Maryland the voter had to have in the county in which he wished to vote a freehold of £50, or personal property of £30. In Virginia the voter had to own twenty-five acres of land of cultivated property, and a house at least twelve feet square on the foundation, or he had to have fifty acres of wild land, or a freehold or estate interest in a lot in some of the towns established by law. In North Carolina the voter had to be a tax-payer. In South Carolina the voter had to be a free white man, acknowledging belief in God and in a future state of reward and punishment, and had to live one year in the state, have a freehold of fifty acres, or own a town lot, or have paid a tax equal to the tax on fifty acres of land. In Georgia any mechanic, any male white inhabitant owning £10 of property and paying a tax not only might vote but had to vote, under penalty of £5.

The estimate of historians is that out of the 4,000,000 of people in the thirteen colonies, including slaves, women and children and other citizens who were non-voters, there were only 150,000 qualified to vote, and therefore we may properly say, that in one sense the people whose delegates and representatives framed the Constitution of the United States were not one twenty-fifth part of all the people of the United States at that time. Judge Sharswood, a great jurist of Pennsylvania, said: "It is to be remarked that in the various

nations, even in the representative government of
the United States, the consent of the entire body
of the people has never been expressed, as 'the
people' comprise all of the women and children
of every age and class.   But they were not 'the
people' in the same sense, until the Constitution
was adopted.   A certain number of men have
assumed to act in the name of all the community."
(1 Sharswood Blackstone, 147 N. 11; 2 Wilson's
Works, 566; Andrew's American Law, Sec. 122.)
Yet the Government of the United States became
the typical popular government of the world and
has been made the chief model of many popular
governments since established.

The political history of each State since the
Constitution was adopted shows a gradual enlarg-
ing of the electorate so as to eliminate religious
and property qualifications, and to reach manhood suffrage.   Until recently the electorate in
each State was limited to males over twenty-one
years and the result has been, as seen in the presidential elections when the vote was the highest,
that the qualified electorate in the United States
has not amounted to more than 20 per cent of
the total population.   If this number is to be
increased by allowing women to vote, it would
probably increase the percentage of the electorate
to 35 or 40 per cent of the total number of the

people resident in the United States. As we must govern by a majority or a plurality of those who have the right to vote, we may properly say that this must always be a government by a minority of all the people of the country.

These are mathematical facts that no one can escape, and it thus appears that there is a large part of the people who are governed and in whose interest government is maintained, to whom it is impossible safely to extend the electoral franchise. No one proposes to do so. No one proposes, for instance, to extend the electoral franchise to children or minors, to aliens who live here and do not wish to be naturalized, to aliens who live here and who can not by law be naturalized, to the insane, or to those who have shown themselves by crime to be unfitted to vote.

These facts do not make against government by the people as we understand it. It only shows that approval of so-called popular government is not worship of a fetish. We are not in favor of the rule of all the people as an end desirable in itself. We love what is called democracy not because of the name but because of what it accomplishes. We are in favor of a rule by as many of the people in a democracy as will secure a good government and no more. The result will be good because it secures the happiness of the individual.

Government is a means to an end, and the means are to be selected on account of their adaptability to the end.

I will illustrate the point I am making if I say that women should be accorded the privilege, and given the duty, of voting, not because they have an inherent and inalienable right to vote, but because, by giving them the franchise, their own welfare or that of the whole body of the people will be thereby promoted. If the advocates of female suffrage can show that they, as a class, have been unjustly prejudiced by governmental measures or by lack of them, and that they could remedy this by their vote, or if they can show that, by the extension of the franchise to women, either the general Government would be better or stronger, or the existing electorate would be improved in its average moral tone, its intelligence, its political discrimination, its patriotism and attention to political duties, they make their case; and they do so because they thus establish that the addition of them to the electorate is a useful means to secure the happiness of the individuals.

While it is impossible to escape the proposition then that we have not a Government by all the people, in the sense that we do not include in those who exercise the power of control all the people, or a majority of them; nevertheless, in fixing our federal franchise we do seek to make our voters in a true sense representative of all the people. The theory of manhood suffrage is that after a man becomes twenty-one he represents in a true sense some of the same class as himself—that is, of those similarly situated—who are related to him. The husband represents his wife; the father the children; the brother the sister, and even though we make our electorate as wide as possible by giving all women of adult age the franchise, we must still have the principle of representative authority in the practical carrying out of popular government.   Jameson Constitutional Conventions, Sect. 335, 336, 337; Andrews' American Law, Sect. 122.

The theory of an original contract between those who made the Government and those who were to live under it, in which each member gave up some so-called natural rights and consented to the exercise of governmental authority, on condition that he enjoyed certain other rights under the protection of the Government, is of course not a true statement of what has happened in history. It was advanced by Rousseau for the basis of a rightful government.   As a working formula the theory is sometimes useful to test the correctness and justice of institutions which are made part of governmental machinery.   When we all theoretically consent to, and actually acquiesce in, a popular government, we say to ourselves, "This is a good government, and we can count on its efficacy, its honesty and its high ideal, and on its practical protection of our rights because the governing body, to wit, the electorate, is composed of citizens of varying intelligence, self-restraint and patriotism, the average of whose political capacity is sufficiently high to justify the belief that the majority will in its political control be fairly wise, prudent and patriotic." Now if we find that the burden involved in the political activity legally required of the average citizen, leads a large number of the electorate and those the more intelligent utterly to neglect their political duty and not to vote, because there are too many elections, or because they feel unfitted to vote on the subjects submitted, with the result that a minority of the electorate of less average intelligence and capacity than the whole is in control, it seems to be clear that the man who is held to consent to this form of government is not receiving the benefit of the government which he had a right to expect.

What is the remedy for this? The Government should either adopt measures which will compel the delinquents to vote, or we must change the law by calling on the electorate for political action less frequently, so that with a lighter burden they may be induced to carry it and give the attention that the interest of the State requires from them in the matter of elections.

Can we meet this difficulty by requiring all the citizens who can cast a vote, to vote, under penalty? This has been attempted in Switzerland and Belgium. I am not fully advised as to the operation of such a law in Belgium, but in Switzerland its result has not been satisfactory. One man can take a horse to water, but fifteen can not make him drink. The men who were compelled to vote in Switzerland on issues referred to them under their referendum law, voted blanks in large percentage, because either they were not interested, or did not feel that they had knowledge enough to express an opinion, or for some other reason. The difficulties as to enforcing such a remedy, therefore, would seem to remit us to the only other one that I know of, which is that we should limit the political duties of the average elector to those which experience shows he is likely to perform. This will prevent too numerous elections. It will lead to a government more representative and less direct, and it will make possible the short ballot, because it will limit the elective offices to a small number and will impose the responsibility of appointment of all other officers upon the few who are elected.

A system which leads to a continuous neglect by a majority of the electorate of their political duties, conclusively shows its unfitness. It is condemned—negatively, it is true, but none the less emphatically—by the very electorate upon whom the safety of the Government depends. The Government becomes one of an active minority. Experience does not show that such a minority is the wisest part of the electorate or the part best adapted to secure good government.

Of course the argument advanced at once is that men who do not care to take part in the government and do not care to discharge their political duties must be regarded as forfeiting their right to do so and must be held responsible for all the ills that come. But the difficulty of this argument is that it ignores altogether the rights of others who do perform their political duties and who vote on every occasion required, and also that large part of the people who are not entitled to vote at all. Both classes have a vital interest in the character of the Government which is imposed on them, and may justly insist that in such a Government it is the general character of the whole electorate that they have a right to rely upon, to secure to them proper and efficient administration and the maintenance of right and justice.

It is altogether an error to assume that a man who neglects his own political duties is only injuring himself. He is injuring everybody who has a right to the exercise by him of his intelligence and experience in the decision of the questions presented to an electorate. It is a just cause of complaint against the laws if they provide electoral duties so heavy that they necessarily discourage his political activity.

Of course the effort should be to strike a mean. It may be necessary, where his duty is light and his neglect of his duty is unreasonable, to institute personal penalties against an elector. But where the practical working of the law is to keep away from the polls a majority of the electors, such penalties would be impracticable, and it is only fair to assume in such a case that the duties imposed are unreasonable and should be entrusted to representatives. When we find, as we often do, in the same election a large vote for candidates and a small vote on legislative issues, it is the best evidence that a majority of the electorate have neither interest nor information enough to lead them to vote on such issues, but do feel themselves competent to select representatives for the purpose.

II

THE REPRESENTATIVE SYSTEM

In my last lecture, I sought to show that we should not worship democracy or the rule of the people as a fetish, that government of any kind is only a means to an end, that the end is the happiness of each individual, and that the reason why we favor popular government is because we believe that it is more effective in securing the happiness of each individual and each class of individuals than any other. I invited your attention to the fact that there is, and can be, no truly popular government, in the sense that all the people have a voice in the government as part of the electorate; that a great many more than a mere majority must always be excluded from the electorate, and this, for the purpose of adapting the government better to the end in view; that on the same ground the political duties of each elector ought to be made light enough to secure the attention and activity of the majority, so that the average intelligence of the electorate may exert its proper influence at the polls, and that a system which wearies the mass of voters and keeps them from the polls is condemned by that fact.

These premises were necessary in my judgment to a proper consideration of the question of the wisdom of the changes in our present government, involved in the adoption of the devices known as "the initiative, the referendum and the recall." These are proposed either as a substitute for, or by way of improving the representative system of, popular government. Before coming to a detailed description and discussion of the new devices, I believe it to be germane and relevant to describe the representative system and to point out why it was adopted and what purpose it served.

Mr. Root, in one of his lectures at Princeton, says of the system:

"The expedient of the representation first found its beginning in the Saxon Witenagemot. It was lost in the Norman conquest. It was restored step by step, through the centuries in which Parliament established its power as an institution through the granting or withholding of aids and taxes for the king's use. It was brought to America by the English colonists. It was the practice of the colonies which formed the Federal Union. It entered into the Constitution as a matter of

course, because it was the method by which
modern liberty had been steadily growing stronger
and broader for six centuries as opposed to the
direct, unrepresentative method of government in
which the Greek and Roman and Italian republics
had failed. This representative system has in its
turn impressed itself upon the nations which
derived their political ideas from Rome and has
afforded the method through which popular
liberty has been winning forward in its struggle
against royal and aristocratic power and privilege the world over. Bluntschli, the great Heidel-
berg publicist of the last century, says:

" 'Representative government and self-government are the great works of the English and
American peoples. The English have produced
representative monarchy with parliamentary
legislation and parliamentary government. The
Americans have produced the representative
republic. We Europeans upon the Continent
recognize in our turn that in representative government alone lies the hoped-for union between
civil order and popular liberty.' "

The problem of popular government is difficult.
In a pure one-man despotism, the machinery is
simple. It needs only to express the will of one
individual. In a limited monarchy in which the

power of government is divided between the King, at the head of the state, and representatives of different classes in the community, it is less easy to frame a satisfactory plan. Finally, when the King and privileged classes are dispensed with, the complications of government are increased. The problem in a popular government is so to arrange its organization that, with due protection to individual and minority rights, which experience has shown to be useful to society and its progress, the expressed will of a majority of an electorate may be truly interpreted and executed in effective action by the government. The business of administering and legislating for a government is not an easy task. Men of experience in governmental affairs and special knowledge are certainly better able to carry it on than those who have neither. In ordinary life, when we wish a man to draft a will, or a contract, or a deed, or some legal document that is to meet legal requirements, we employ a lawyer. When we would have a member of our family who is ill attended by anyone, we employ a physician. When we would have our children educated, we employ professional teachers. When we wish to build a bridge or a road, we employ professional engineers. When we would build a house, we employ an architect and a competent contractor and carpenter. When "We, the

people," have an object in view, we are generally
lacking in the knowledge and practical experience
to devise a practical measure to secure it. It
would seem wise on our part to employ in such
matters men who have the special knowledge and
experience enabling them by amendment and discussion to shape measures that will receive the
judicial interpretation that we wish to have them
bear, and to employ others who know how to
enforce them.

Take the question of currency and banking.
We know generally that we would like to have a
currency issued under a plan automatic in operation, by which the volume shall increase to meet
the wants of trade in times of prosperity and
expansion, and shall be reduced when the conditions of business require less. If there is too little
currency in circulation at times when the timidity
of people lead them to hoard it, we are likely to
have a money panic that causes a disastrous halt
in business, and if, at other times, we have too
much idle currency, its unnecessary volume may
lead to unhealthy speculation and unwise investments. In drafting such a law and its enactment,
we should have men representing us in Congress
who by reason of their experience and their studies
and their discussions and their knowledge of
government finance and banking can properly

prepare, discuss and enact the law. It is obviously impossible for the electorate of fifteen millions to meet together and to deliberate with any hope of reaching a satisfactory conclusion as to such legislation.

As government increases in its functions—and the tendency of modern times is to increase the variety of the functions of government—the necessity for the employment of agents who have a specialized knowledge in carrying out such new governmental functions is much greater than where the office of government was limited, as Jefferson would have limited it, largely to the preservation of order and the administration of justice—that is, to a simple police system. What is true in respect to legislation is equally true as to the selection of governmental administrators to execute the laws. In the maintenance of a modern government, it is necessary to employ a vast number of public agents. In the Federal Government, the number runs up into the hundreds of thousands. Now it is obviously impossible for the 15,000,000 of voters, or a majority of that body, carefully and intelligently to select the hundreds of thousands of those who are to execute the laws and the general policy determined by an election. Therefore, our Constitution provides for the appointment of all of these officers, and that chiefly by the President, who, representing all the people, does the best he can to secure good appointees.

This is a representative democracy, in the sense that the people ultimately govern, but they make their government effective by the use of competent agents whom they elect as their representatives.

What the duty of the representative is, of course, has always been a subject of discussion. Undoubtedly when a man permits his name to be submitted to the people as a candidate for their suffrages, with the announcement, either by himself or through a party, that he is in favor of certain governmental policies to be embodied in executive or legislative action, he is bound to conform to those policies or is guilty of deceit. But in the discharge of the functions of a representative, it often occurs that issues arise which were not the subject of discussion at the time of the election, and it often occurs also that even though the general object was the subject of discussion, the particular means to be selected furnished so complicated a question that it played no part in the election. Under such circumstances, I conceive that the representative is to act on his own best judgment, even though it may differ from that of many of his constituents.

This was the view that Edmund Burke took, as

shown in his letter to his Bristol constituents. Indeed, Burke went further and insisted that a member of Parliament elected by a district, when elected, ceased to be the representative of the people of that district only and became a representative of the whole Kingdom. I fully concur in that view. Members of Congress owe their allegiance first to the people of the whole community whenever there is a difference between the interest of the country and that of the district. The representative ought not to be the mere mouthpiece of his constituents. He is elected because presumably he is well fitted to discharge the particular duties in respect to which he is to occupy a representative capacity, and he knows more about them than his constituents. In carrying out their general purpose, in accord with his promise, he is still within his authority if he selects his own means of executing that promise according to his conscience.

Again, popular government is impossible without parties. If you have 15,000,000 voters, and every voter is going to have a different view, or every voter differs from every other voter on something, and so they do not agree politically on anything, you will have a chaos that will result in simple negation. In a proper system of party government, the members of each party must agree on certain main doctrines in respect to governmental policy and yield their views on the less important ones, in order that they may have united action, and in order that these main and controlling doctrines, when the party is successful at the election and controls the Government, may furnish the guide for governmental action. But parties can not be organized and can not give expression to their views without having leaders, captains, lieutenants and file leaders, without taking the advice of those leaders, and without being influenced by their leadership.

Parties thus in turn adopt the representative system, and the people of the parties appoint delegates to conventions that are supposed to express the party will in the selection of candidates and the declaration of principles. The leaders of the party, the delegates who represent the people of the party, meeting in convention, are charged with the responsibility of nominating fit men for office and of adopting principles that will unify the party and will properly appeal for the support of the entire people.

This is the way in which our representative government down to within a few years has been carried on, not only in the general Government, in the State governments, but also in the organization and maintenance of parties; and there are

but few who will not admit that theoretically it is
a plan admirably adapted to the creation of
efficient government by competent representatives, carrying out in good faith the general purposes of the party which has received the mandate
of government from the majority of the electorate.

We have had 125 years of this system, but now
we are told that it has failed, and that either it
must be changed in a radical way and abolished,
or else it must have a supplement which shall
correct its evils and give to the people and all the
people a more direct control of the laws passed,
and of the executive action taken. What is the
reason and what the necessity for this change?
I wish to be as fair as I can in the statement of the
arguments in its behalf. Many books have been
written to show the growth of capitalistic control, by corrupt means, of State legislatures and
other local tribunals in which and through which
charters and special privileges have been voted.
They set out in detail the political influences
which railroad and other great public utility companies have been able to exercise in politics.
From 1865, immediately after the war, until 1900,
there was a remarkable expansion of population
and commerce. The movement did not take place
in the South until the eighties, or later, but cer-

tain it is that from 1880 to 1900, in the prosperity and expansion that manifested itself on every hand, the whole attention of nearly all the people was devoted to commercialism. I remember in 1878 when I was graduated from Yale College, the Class of 1853 had its twenty-fifth anniversary, and President Andrew D. White, of Cornell, a member of the class, delivered an address. He took for his subject "The Commercial Spirit," and he prophesied, if it were to continue unabated, the evils which have come. By seizing the opportunities which the corporation laws in various States offered, combinations were increased and added to, and became, in the flush times of the McKinley Administration, after the hard times of the Cleveland Administration, all commanding in business, in politics, and, it would seem, in society. I am the last one to minimize the critical nature of the conditions which prevailed in politics and business and society after the Spanish War, and which seemed to have crystallized into a rigid control of all by great business combinations which could not be shaken. Then there arose a protest, or rather a chorus of protests, which called public attention to the danger that was confronting the people and their government in the control of those artificial creations of the law which circumstances had fostered and permitted to grow into Frankensteins as they were. Leaders arose and led a popular crusade to destroy the undue power of wealth in politics, and to bring these great quasi-public corporations within the regulative influence of legislative and executive action.

The indignant spirit of the people thus aroused is what has prompted the demand for a change from a representative government to one in which the people are to act directly and immediately in legislative and executive matters. That the occasion for the general alarm was justified, no one who has studied the situation can deny. That we were thus saved from the continued corrupt and subterranean control of legislatures and other depositaries of the privilege-granting power, every careful observer must admit. We should rejoice as patriots from the bottom of our hearts for this popular rising, even though it has projected these new questions into politics and has for the time being raised queries as to the wisdom of our present form of government. The inconveniences and the possible excesses which may come from the rousing to action of a leviathan like the people are inevitable. The advantage derived from their quickened conscience, however, is worth all the incidental mistakes or injustice that may be done, before the sobering effect of experience produces a reaction carrying conditions back, not to the abuses of old, but to that point where the original movement might wisely have ended.

The initiative, referendum and recall were proposed in order to clinch the reform I have been describing. It was thought that they were instrumentalities which would prevent forever a recurrence of the abuses. This result, if it could be attained, would certainly be real progress. The advocates of these new institutions, confident of their efficacy, therefore denominated them as progressive measures, and themselves as Progressives.

There is another form of progressivism which calls for notice here. It has grown out of the conditions I have referred to, and operates not only upon the collective conscience of the public but also upon that of individuals who have come to see clearly the folly of devoting themselves exclusively to the mad chase for money and to realize the greater happiness they can attain in making themselves useful to their less fortunate brethren. The accumulated wealth has created a leisure class that recognizes, in the opportunity that their circumstances afford, a responsibility to society to lessen the burden and suffering of the poor and the oppressed under our present economic and social system, and render opportunities for self-betterment in society more nearly equal. There has arisen, as a reaction from the commercial spirit, a greater social consciousness. The organization of social settlements, the expansion and increased effectiveness of charitable organizations and the greater social responsibility of men of wealth—already alluded to—manifest a stimulated fraternity of feeling among members of society toward each other.

This has led to a demand for increasing the functions of Government to relieve the oppressed and the less fortunate in society. The *laissez faire* school would have opposed such functions as paternalistic. Undoubtedly, the Government can wisely do much more than that school would have favored to relieve the oppressed, to create greater equality of opportunity, to make reasonable terms for labor in employment, and to furnish vocational education of the children of the poor. But on the other hand, there is a line beyond which Government can not go with any good practical results in seeking to make men and society better. Efforts to do so will only result in failure and a waste of public effort and funds. But many enthusiasts, whose whole attention has been so centered on the poverty and suffering in cities or elsewhere as to lead them to disregard the general average improvement of the individual in the com-

munity in comfort of life and happiness, have lost
their sense of due proportion and spend their
energies in pressing forward legislative plans for
the uplift of the suffering and the poor and for
the mulcting of the fortunate, the thrifty and the
well-to-do that are impracticable and will only
result in defeat, and increased burden of taxation.
This attitude in favor of such measures among
the well-to-do, and the propaganda they have
made in unjust denunciation of general social and
economic conditions, have found ready response in
the classes among whom penury, want and misfortune exist.

The elements I have been describing have
worked together to produce a school of political
philosophers and a large group of followers who
call for a change in the fundamental structure of
our Government which shall give to the majority
of those voting immediate and direct control of
new legislation and immediate and direct power to
remove all limitations which the fundamental law
may present, with a view to the adoption of legislation supposed to be needed to carry out the
three purposes: first, to prevent the corruption of
politics by corporate wealth; second, to further
equality of opportunity, to alleviate penury, want
and social and economic inequalities and injustices, and third, to change or qualify the right of

property so as more nearly to equalize property conditions.

The plans of this new school of progressives involve much in their general purposes that all good men sympathize with; but the methods they propose and the bitter class spirit they encourage are dangerous in the extreme, and if carried to their logical result will undermine just and enduring popular government. We all sympathize deeply with a purpose to destroy the possibility of plutocracy and we welcome the quickened social consciousness, but because we object to the proposed remedies, and insist that they are sure to fail and will lose for all the people the solid foundation for safe progress in our present form of government, we are relegated to the position of reactionaries, and of men who do not sympathize with progress. Those of us who are thus unjustly classed must be content to be so until vindicated by the event. But we must fight for our principles and maintain them without fear, because unless we do, as I verily believe, our form of representative democracy will be destroyed and its power to aid and maintain the happiness of the individual will cease.

There is nothing to show that all legitimate governmental purposes sought by the so-called Progressives may not be promoted and brought about under the representative system. Admitting that it may be somewhat more slow in its results, it will insure wiser action in detail because of greater deliberation. Great reforms should not be brought about overnight. They need time. They should be marked by careful consideration.

It is said that the representative system is a failure because it gave rise to these evils. Of course the evils did come and they came under the representative system, and it is true that, in the working out of the political evils, politicians adopted means which were fitted to succeed under the representative system. But it does not follow that politicians might not, if we had the other system, address themselves to its weaknesses and bring about a result quite as disheartening. The truth is that what we all utterly ignore in the growth of the abuses which have given rise to this demand for a change in the structure of the government is that the real defect, deeper down than mere machinery, was the sluggishness of the people and a sort of tacit sympathy of the people with those who were promoting the expansion and the material progress of the country in which the people expected to share. People voted without hesitation bonds for the construction of a railroad equal to many thousand dollars a mile, to be paid for by the county or some other local subdivision, in order to secure better transportation in that vicinity. Then when the railroad was built, and the people had to pay the bonds, the whole public attitude was changed and the bitterest antagonism to the railroad company was shown. This is human nature. First, in order to resist injustice, then to acquire unjust advantage, the railroads and other franchise holders used corrupt means. The continued success of such methods with state legislatures and municipal councils was possible only because of the original sympathy of the people with those building up the country by their investments and enterprises, and of their unwillingness at that time to devote proper care to their political duties in selecting and watching legislators and councilmen. In other words, instead of blaming the character of the representative system for recent conditions, we must put the blame where it belongs and not upon a system of government that has stood the test of experience for centuries as the best and wisest means for giving effect to the popular will. Of course, the means used to make corruption successful for a time were cunningly adapted to take advantage of the prominent features of the representative system. The promoters of corruption used the party convention and the party caucus to further their purpose, and they deceived the people as to the character of their candidates. They might have to change their methods under the proposed changes to a more direct democracy, but if the people neglect their duties in politics the same manipulators could learn to turn the new system to their use quite as successfully as the old.

There is no warrant for the assertion that the representative system can not be made to serve the purposes of honest government and of legislative and executive reforms just as well as the new devices proposed.

One of the strongest reasons for saying so is what has happened. With the heart of our people sound and honest, the dishonesty of their agents has awakened them. Under the influence of their awakening a wonderful change has taken place in every legislative body in the country, and reform laws, many of them meritorious and useful, have been promptly enacted. Indeed, even where the initiative, referendum and recall have been adopted under this impulse, it had to be done through purely representative government machinery.

If this was the case then, why condemn the representative system as not sufficiently responsive to the will of the people when aroused to action?

But it is said that the people will be lulled to inertia again, and then the corruptionists and the politicians will again be working their evil schemes and binding the people as the Lilliputians bound Gulliver. This is certainly inconsistent with the widespread announcement that there is a permanently aroused public and an awakened social conscience. I am glad to believe that the people have learned a permanent lesson from bitter experience in the necessity for holding their representatives strictly responsible for protecting the public in all forms of public grants, whether of money, property, franchises or privileges. I hope to be able to show that the new devices are more likely to produce neglect of the voting part of the people to attend to their duties than this representative system under which, by the method of what is known as a short ballot, we can lessen the electoral duties of the people and secure their general attention at moderate intervals for concentrated and effective action.

III

The Initiative and the Referendum

I now come to the consideration of the system which it is proposed to substitute for the representative system. The new system embraces three parts: the referendum, the initiative and the recall. Let us take them in their order. The referendum, speaking generally, is nothing but a reference of an issue to a decision by a popular election. It has long been known in the political machinery of this Government, and has long been used for certain purposes; and while its operation has not been entirely satisfactory, it seems the only feasible plan to accomplish that for which it is used.

In the first place, after a proposed constitutional amendment has been formulated, discussed, amended and modified in some deliberative assembly, like a constitutional convention or legislature, and has been recommended for adoption by the convention or legislature, or, as some constitutions provide, after it has twice received such examination and favorable vote at successive legislative sessions, it is then submitted to the people for them to determine, by a majority vote, whether it is to be finally adopted. Under some systems a constitutional amendment is not adopted unless a majority of all those voting at the election shall vote for it. Under other systems, it is enough if a majority of those voting on the issue shall be in its favor. Of course, if there is no other issue pending at the election, and there are no candidates running for office, then a majority of those voting at the election and a majority of those voting on an issue are the same, but often at such elections candidates for office are voted for, and it has usually resulted that the votes for candidates are largely in excess of those cast on a constitutional issue. The difference, therefore, between a majority of those voting at the election and those voting on the issue is generally a very material one. I have no hesitancy in saying that I think the requirement that the vote should be a majority of those voting at the election is the safer and better one. In Minnesota the former rule prevails and some four or five amendments proposed have failed, though more voted for them than against them, because the favorable vote was not a majority of the total vote cast for candidates for office at the same election. It too often happens, as we shall see, that the vote on constitutional issues thus taken awakens so little interest that the total vote on the issue is hardly more than half the usual vote cast for candidates for office. The total vote *pro* and *con* on the issue is hardly a majority of the electorate, and a majority of those voting is thus a comparatively small minority of the whole electorate. The constitution is the fundamental law adopted after deliberation, discussion and final vote of the people. It embodies the self-imposed restraint by the people upon those who act for them in passing laws or executing laws or policies. Those solemnly enacted restraints that have been tried for years, and upon the faith of which so much of business and individual action has been based, should not be lightly changed, certainly not by less than a majority of the electorate. The small vote by which in some States the most marked changes are brought about in their constitutions, does not show the stability in our Government which we were wont to think we had, and which gave us such pride in the proven efficacy and permanence of popular rule. Thus in California the vote which carried most radical amendments to the constitution, with changes of immense importance in the structural framework of the State government, was considerably less than that of the vote a year before cast for the minority candidate for the Presidency, who lost the State by sixty thousand (60,000) and it was less than one-third of the total vote for the Presidency. In Ohio there were forty-one different constitutional changes voted on at a special election in September, 1912. The total vote was very little more than 500,000, ·and the prevailing vote was generally less than 300,000. In the November following the total vote was over 1,100,000, showing that these radical constitutional changes were effected by less than 30 per cent of those electors who turned out at a presidential election and considerably less than 25 per cent of the total electorate. I have already pointed out how important it is that a large part of the electorate shall discharge their duties, and how unfair it is that so large a proportion of the electors avoid elections when they concern the adoption of legislative or constitutional changes. Still, under the systems that have prevailed, preliminaries are required of a character to advise the whole people of the issue, and delays are enforced to secure deliberation. Thus in the process of adopting such constitutional amendments, the final action of the people has usually been preceded by the detailed discussion, in a deliberative assembly like a legislature or a convention, of every clause and by the proposal of amendments of every clause for the purpose of betterment.   The public are advised of the character of the amendments by the discussion in the assembly or convention, and substantial time elapses in which to enable the public to acquire knowledge of what is proposed in the change of fundamental law.   Sometimes, indeed, two years are consumed in the necessary preliminaries for a constitutional amendment.   Where, however, the referendum is associated with the initiative, we shall see that no such safeguards are provided to give the public the benefit of amendment by persons of experience or of time for information and deliberation.

Second, the referendum has been used for years as a condition upon which local legislation enacted by a state legislature shall go into effect.   For instance, when the question is whether a prohibition law ought to be put into operation in a municipality, district or county, it has become frequently the custom on the part of the legislatures to provide that the law shall go into operation in such municipality, district or county, if, in a local election, a majority of the voters lawfully residing therein shall vote in favor of its operation—otherwise not.   This is what is called the local option arrangement, and has the advantage of making the going into effect of the law depend upon the question whether it can be really

enforced.   Experience has shown that a law of
this kind, sumptuary in its character, can only be
properly enforced in districts in which a majority
of the people favor the law, and, therefore, favor
its enforcement; but in a district where the
majority of the people are opposed to the law,
and do not sympathize with its provisions, a
sumptuary law is almost certain to become a dead
letter. Now every one must recognize the demoralizing effect of the enactment of laws and their
attempted enforcement and their failure because
of the lack of public opinion to support the officers
of the law in attempting such enforcement.
It ought to be said that localities have interest
enough in such a local question as liquor selling to
make the vote much nearer that on candidates
in a general election.   The issue is simple and
thoroughly understood, it is sharp, and the people
know their minds.

Attempts have been made in courts to impeach
the constitutionality of a referendum law like
this, on the theory that the legislature can not
delegate its legislative power to the people without special constitutional authority.   Courts have
sustained the law, however, on the theory that the
legislation was the act of the legislature, and that
the legislature had the authority to impose such
conditions as to its going into effect as the legis-

lature might choose, and that the question of the referendum and the issue in the referendum were nothing but the conditions upon which the law was to go into effect.

The referendum has been used in other cases. Wherever the local legislative body has the power to act in such a conclusive way that the people are unable by electing a successor to reverse the action, it is a security against precipitate or corrupt action to require that there shall be a referendum before the action of the local body becomes effective. Thus where the legislature authorizes a city council to issue bonds, binding the municipality to pay a large debt twenty or thirty years hence, in such an important matter as this, the approval of the people may well be had. And so in the issuing of franchises to corporations that may not be amended or revoked, for the same reason the opinion of the people may usefully be invited on the question of the grant before it becomes binding. I may add that in such cases also, the questions thus referred are simple and easily understood and the people can vote with a clear idea of what the election means.

The new school of political philosophers proposes the referendum for far wider uses than I have described. It will be observed, in the instances I have mentioned, that the use of the referendum was voluntary, that is, the legislature could invoke its use but they were not compelled to do so. The new theory, however, is that we are to have a compulsory referendum, that the legislature shall be compelled to refer all laws of importance to the people, and that this referendum may be effected, without the intervention of the legislature at all, but through another instrumentality which I have mentioned, to wit, the initiative. By the initiative is meant an institution under which a certain percentage of the voters signing and filing a petition in some named state office, are enabled to require the state authorities to submit for adoption, by referendum to the lawful voters of the State, any bill for enactment into law of which the petitioners set forth a copy in their petition. The percentage of the registered voters required to make such a petition effective in many of the States is 5 per cent; in others 8 per cent, and in some others is higher, but 8 per cent is usually the requirement. Under this system, as it is actually employed in a great many States, legislation of the most complicated character, embodied in bills, numbering as high as thirty-five or forty, has been submitted at one regular election to the people for their consideration and adoption. In such cases, if the people by a vote of a majority of those voting on each issue shall favor the proposed legislation, it becomes law, and this without being subject to a veto by the Governor or to any interference or change by the legislature.

The question is whether this system is one that ought to approve itself to the public for general adoption. It is argued that, in this way, subterranean influences of corrupt character can be avoided because the whole electorate can not be corrupted. It is argued that in this way prompt action is secured in deference to popular will, and that legislation, beneficial to the public and avoiding or abolishing special privilege, can not be obstructed or prevented by the hugger-muggering of political bosses acting under the inspiration of corrupt corporate managers.

I do not mean to say that in the early use of such a device as this upon legislation, the results may not seem to be more directly under the control of the people than under the representative system when it was being used and abused by corrupt methods. However, the ease with which the so-called pure democracy can be turned to the advantage of the corruptionist has yet to be shown. His opportunity will be in the failure of the majority of the people to perform their heavier political duty under the new system, and human nature has greatly changed if such opportunity will not be improved. With the legislatures now in the chastened condition to which the indignation of the people has brought them, they are not any less responsive in respect of legislation which the people desire than the people themselves. More than this, the great advantage under the representative system is that it gives room for intelligent discussion and amendment, whereas under the initiative and referendum such opportunity for bettering the proposal and making it practical and useful is wholly wanting. Under the initiative, those who sign a petition frame the bill just as they wish to have it, and then the public must accept or reject it. To such an audience as this, it is hardly necessary to point out the fact that, in the history of legislative measures, the original bill is often so changed and perfected for the good of the public, and to promote the real and beneficial object, that the bill as introduced can hardly be recognized in the bill as passed. The bill as passed accomplishes its purpose, because it has been made over by men whose knowledge fits them to frame legislation to accomplish a particular purpose, while the original bill is quite likely to have been impracticable and a failure. The opportunity for amendment is one of the most important steps in securing proper laws.

Again: Representative government is said to be a failure because the people are not capable of selecting proper representatives, and yet the whole system of referendum and initiative rests upon the assumed intelligence and discretion of the people, sufficient to pass upon the wisdom of the details of thirty complicated bills at one election. The official explanation of these bills in fine print filled a pamphlet of 300 pages. Now I submit whether the people as a whole may not more certainly select honest and intelligent agents to act for them in considering and adopting such difficult legislative measures than they can exercise a discriminating and intelligent choice in respect to the approval or disapproval of such measures. I commend a perusal of the laws submitted to the electors of Oregon at the last general election, and if the reader does not lay down the book containing them with fatigue, confused mind, tired eyes and a disgusted feeling, I am mistaken. If it has that effect on the reader, consider how much more tired and confused the perceptions of the voter of average intelligence must be. It is not too much to say that only a small percentage have the patience to read through the proposed bills, much less the knowledge and persistence to learn what they mean and decide upon their effect and value.

We have had societies organized by conscientious reformers for the purpose of simplifying issues at an election. The platforms of various organizations have approved what is called the short ballot. Now, what is the principle of the short ballot? What does it mean? It means that the number of electoral offices to be voted on by the people shall be reduced to as few as possible, and that all other offices shall be filled by appointment by the few to be elected, so that the persons elected may be held responsible by the people, and the people may, by selecting a few honest and intelligent agents, be sure that all the other officers to be appointed will be selected with a care, knowledge and discrimination that the people have not the means of exercising. Now if that is a reform that ought to be adopted, does it not necessarily follow that the submission to the people of such matters of complicated legislation as have been offered to the voters of Oregon and the other States where the voters at a general election are invited to pass upon a very volume of proposed laws, is directly in the teeth of the principle upon which the short ballot is founded? Is not the advocacy of the short ballot a conclusive admission that a system by which a small percentage can foist upon an unoffending electorate the burden of passing on complicated and voluminous legislation is to be avoided? An examination of a ballot in Oregon, or in South Dakota, or in Colorado, yards long and feet wide, will at once convince any reasonable man that the system which makes such a ballot possible is a travesty upon practical methods of ascertaining the deliberate will of the people either in legislation or in the selection of candidates.

Again, the people themselves have indicated that they are far better able to select candidates than they are to pass upon complicated questions of legislation, and they have done so by the withholding of expression of any opinion at all upon these many legislative issues that have been submitted to them in the same elections where they have in full numbers expressed their opinion on the selection of candidates for office. This very act of the people themselves shows that they think that the intricate legislative issues submitted are not proper questions to be submitted to a popular election. Could any system be devised better adapted to the exaltation of cranks and the wearying of the electorate of their political duties than the giving of power to 5 per cent or even 8 per cent of the voters to submit all the fads and nostrums that their active but impractical minds can devise, to be voted on in frequent elections? They invented this initiative in Switzerland and when a considerable percentage of voters refused to vote on the issues presented, they imposed a fine for failure to vote, with the result that the voters, to avoid the fine, cast their ballots, but they were blank. Examine the record in referendum states and you will find that the total vote on legislative referendums varies from 75 per cent to 25 per cent of the votes cast for candidates at the same election.

I have a letter from Governor Buchtel of Colorado, chancellor of the University of Denver, in respect to the initiative and referendum in Colorado and Denver, which was written in response to my inquiry as to how the system was working there. It is as follows:

"UNIVERSITY OF DENVER,

Denver, Colo., April 25, 1913.

My dear Friend:

I send you herewith report on two state elections and two city elections, held recently, in which the actual vote for initiated measures is shown in connection with the available vote. It is all very depressing. We changed our form of government here in the city of Denver with a total vote of 26,842, when the available vote was somewhere between 65,000 and 70,000. The fact is that our people are disgusted with these pro-

grams and so they do not vote at all. We had a
day for registration yesterday.

Most faithfully in high regard,

Henry A. Buchtel.

The General Election was held on November 5,
1912.

The vote for Presidential Electors was   265,991
Average for other officers about . . 260,000

The votes on Initiated Measures at this same
election were as follows:

Initiated Constitutional Amendment
  for State-wide Prohibition:

For	75,877
Against	116,774
Total	192,651

Initiated Constitutional Amendment.
  Recall from Office:

For	53,620
Against	39,564
Total	93,184

Initiated Constitutional Amendment.
Recall of Judicial Decisions:

For	55,416
Against	40,891
Total	96,307

Referred State Law.
Building Moffat Tunnel:

For	45,800
Against	93,183
Total	138,983

CITY OF DENVER ELECTION, MAY 21, 1912

The vote for Mayor was	71,922

Charter Amendment:

Playground Commission, total	34,403

Charter Amendment:

Mountain Parks, total	37,119

Charter Amendment:

Liquor Question, total	34,096

CITY ELECTION, FEBRUARY 14, 1913

The actual vote over most serious matters was:
Telephone Ordinance:

For	25,784
Against	3,315
Total	29,099

Holding Charter Convention to adopt Non-Partisan Commission form of Government:

For	7,632
Against	15,647
Total	23,279

Initiated Measure to give Immediate Non-Partisan Commission form of Government:

For	15,841
Against	11,001
Total	26,842

Non-Partisan System of Election:

For	15,601
Against	11,012
Total	26,613"

Again, in the city of Cleveland, Ohio, the immensely important question whether they should approve a new charter was submitted and resulted as follows:

Registered electors	97,000
For charter	24,037
Against charter	12,077
Not voting	60,886

The charter was thus approved by less than one fourth of electors. It was the result of four months' work of fifteen commissioners.

Such instances might be cited in great number. But it is said by the proposers of this new system, "we propose to teach the people the problems of government and to interest them in matters that they ought to understand. We believe that by continuing we shall ultimately succeed in securing the action of a large majority of the electorate." It is enough to say this has not been the result whenever the attempt to have people vote on complicated legislative measures has been tried. Their interest has decreased. They have been tired and have avoided voting. Is it not much easier to rouse them to their duty to vote only between long intervals and then for a few competent representatives? If education of the people is necessary to make the new system work, does it not seem the course of common sense to retain the old system in which the lesson to be learned is so much simpler and so much more easily taught?

We live in an age of reform—I hope of real reform, but the sham reformers and the crank reformers, the men who have no practical sense with reference to what reform is, will seize upon an opportunity like this initiative to bring the

people to the polls so often, and to increase the
questions to be submitted at the polls to such
number as utterly to disgust the voting public,
and ultimately to reduce the numbers of those
who do vote on such issues to a point where a very
small minority can carry them. Now is this wise?
Is it not turning over our Government to the
cranks? Is it not giving the decision whether
nostrums shall go into operation to the very
inventors of those nostrums? When the careful
student of history shall read over the legislative
measures proposed by the initiative for referendum in the various States and the steps taken
under them, his amazed interest, on one hand, and
his humor, on the other, will all be roused, as ours
now is, by considering the wild propositions that
were made and seriously entertained and for a
time put into operation during the French Revolution.

One of the features of present-day politics is
the lively fear that those engaged in executing the
laws and enacting them entertain of temporary
popular condemnation and criticism. The man
from whom the people really secure the best service is the man who acts on his own judgment as
to what is best for his country and for the people,
even though this be contrary to the temporary
popular notion or passion. The men who are

really the great men of any legislative body are
those who, having views of their own, defend them
and support them, even at the risk of rousing a
popular clamor against themselves.

Take an instance recently noted in the dis-
patches from Washington. A member of the
House has justified making incomes of $4,000 a
year exempt from the proposed national income
tax on the ground that, if the line of immunity
were reduced to incomes of $1,000 and less, it
would create such an opposition to the tax that it
would defeat the party responsible for passing it.
If an income tax is a good thing, and ought to be
imposed, then the line of immunity ought not to be
determined by the question how many votes it
would drive away from the controlling party, or
by the justice and economic wisdom of the limitation. Personally, it seems to me that the lower
the line of immunity the better, from the standpoint of public policy. In all the nations of
Europe the immunity is below the line of $1,000
incomes, and the advantage of this is that it makes
as many as possible contribute something directly
to the Government, and such a contribution rouses
an interest on the part of the tax-payer in the
expenditures of Government, and gives him a
motive for being economical and for wishing to
reduce governmental expenditures as much as

possible. But if the great majority of the voting
population pay no taxes at all, and the taxes are
paid by the comparatively few, then the great
majority in supporting or voting appropriations
of the Government are unaffected by the expenditures and have no sense of responsibility as to
their amount. The reason given by the member
of Congress, whom I have quoted, sufficiently illustrates my point that Congressmen do not permit
themselves to think independently on subjects
entrusted to their judgment and action, but they
keep their eyes constantly on the question of how
the votes of the people may be affected by such
legislation toward the authors of it.

No one ought to minimize the danger there is
of corrupt corporate control of legislatures and
obstruction to popular will. These are serious
evils to be provided against, I fully admit, but, on
the other hand, I think that the slavish subordi-
nation of the representative, against his better
judgment, to temporary, popular passion is also
a serious evil. The disposition of politicians to
coddle the people, to flatter them into thinking
that they can not make a mistake, and to fail to
tell them the truth as to their own errors and
tendencies to error, is a growing difficulty in the
matter of successful popular government. The
assumption that all the defects in our body politic

and social which have manifested themselves are due to the machinations of wicked men, and are not due in any degree to the fault of the people in discharging their political obligations, is a misrepresentation of the truth, but flattering to the people. Ultimately the people learn the truth; ultimately they see through the hypocrisies of those who flatter them, and without hesitation they reverse their action, although it seems as if the entire population had been irrevocably committed to its wisdom. If some of our politicians pursued the course of telling the truth at all hazards to the people about themselves, and about those who wish to mislead them, they might not lose as many votes as they fear.

To all these objections, which seem to me to constitute conclusive reasons against this proposed return to direct government, the answer is: "We do not intend to destroy representative government. We value it highly. We wish merely to better it and make it more responsive to the people's will." The effect of the initiative and referendum upon the legislative branch of the Government, even if it be retained, is necessarily to minimize its power, to take away its courage and independence of action, to destroy its sense of responsibility and to hold it up as unworthy of confidence. Nothing would more certainly destroy the character of a law-making body. No one with just pride and proper self-respect would aspire to a position in which the sole standard of action must be the question what the majority of the electorate, or rather a minority likely to vote, will do with measures the details of which there is neither time nor proper means to make the public understand. The necessary result of the compulsory referendum following the initiative is to nullify and defeat the very advantages of the representative system which made it an improvement upon direct government.

The strongest objection to these instruments of direct government, however, is the effect of their constant use in eliminating all distinction between a constitution as fundamental law, and statutes enacted for the disposition of current matters. When exactly the same sanction, without any greater formalities or deliberation, is given to a statute as to a constitution, to an appropriation bill as to a bill of rights, so that the one may be repealed as easily as the other, the peculiar office of a constitution ceases to be. It minimizes the sacredness of those fundamental provisions securing the personal rights of the individual against the unjust aggression of the majority of the electorate.

We are told by this new school of political

thinkers that there are no inalienable rights of an individual which the people may not, in the interest of the people and the government at large modify, impair or abolish. The contention is that a man has no rights, independent of the will of the people with whom he lives, that he does not inherently possess personal liberty, the right to property, the right to freedom of religion, the right to free speech or that protection secured to him under the title of "due process of law," and that these can be taken from him by legislative or executive action, if sanctioned by a popular vote, with the same ease and dispatch that the repeal of any ordinary law could be effected. Now this is a very different doctrine from that which our forefathers laid down in the Declaration of Independence and exemplified in the provisions of our Constitution and the amendments called "the Bill of Rights" which immediately followed its adoption.

I don't know that a discussion would be productive of much good as to whether such rights are in the moral sense inalienable. I don't care whether they are called inherent rights, or whether it is conceded, as it must be conceded, that experience has shown that in the use of popular government for the promotion of the happiness of the individual and of society, these things which are called rights must be accorded to the individual, if government is to attain the great end of government. In Loan Association vs. Topeka, 1874, 20 Wall, 655, Mr. Justice Miller, speaking for the Supreme Court, used this language:

"A government which recognizes no such rights, which held the lives, the liberty and the property of its citizens subject at all times to the absolute disposition and unlimited control of even the most democratic depository of power, is after all, but a despotism. It is true it is a despotism of the many, of the majority, if you choose to call it so, but it is none the less a despotism. It may well be doubted if a man is to hold all that he is accustomed to call his own, all in which he has placed his happiness, and the security of which is essential to that happiness, under the unlimited dominion of others, whether it is not wiser that this power should be exercised by one man than by many."

The great heritage and glory of the American people has been that their English ancestors first invented representative government and first established these individual rights as against their kings. When, as Americans, they came to establish a government of their own in this country, they developed even more perfectly the representative system and recognized the possibility and probability of error and mistake on the part of themselves in their temporary action, and they therefore imposed upon themselves, and upon their agencies represented in their government, certain limitations in protection of the individual and of the minority. They saw a possible tyranny in a majority in popular government quite as dangerous as the despotism of kings and they prepared a written constitution intended to preserve individual rights against its exercise. It is this fundamental law of popular self-restraint that has aroused the admiration of the world, has commanded the praise of those historians who have studied governments and has led them to the conclusion that it was this that has given such stability and success to the American nation. Lord Acton, one of the greatest historical authorities of any age, in speaking of the Constitution of the United States, said:

"It established a pure democracy, but it was democracy in its highest perfection, armed and vigilant, less against aristocracy and monarchy than against its own weakness and excess. Whilst England was admired for the safeguards with which, in the course of many centuries, it had

fortified liberty against the power of the crown,
America appeared still more worthy of admiration
for the safeguards which, in the deliberations of a
single memorable year, it had set up against the
power of its own sovereign people. It resembled
no other known democracy for it respected freedom, authority and law. It resembled no other
constitution, for it was contained in half a dozen
intelligible articles. Ancient Europe opened its
mind to two new ideas—that revolution with very
little provocation may be just and that democracy
in very large dimensions may be safe."

Now it is proposed to dispense with all the limitations upon legislation contained in the Constitution, and it is proposed to leave to the initiative
and the referendum, without regard to the character of the law, or what it affects, and without
limitation as to individual rights, the absolute
power to legislate according to the will of the
people. This was the principle that prevailed in
the pure democracies of ancient times, and we
know with what disastrous results.

The same great historical authority, Lord
Acton, describes it as follows:

"The philosophy that was then in the ascendant
taught them that there is no law superior to that
of the State—the lawgiver is above the law.

"It followed that the sovereign people had a right to do whatever was within its power, and was bound by no rule of right or wrong but its own judgment of expediency. On a memorable occasion the assembled Athenians declared it monstrous that they should be prevented from doing whatever they chose. No force that existed could restrain them; and they resolved that no duty should restrain them, and that they would be bound by no laws that were not of their own making. In this way the emancipated people of Athens became a tyrant; and their Government, the pioneer of European freedom, stands condemned with a terrible unanimity by all the wisest of the ancients. They ruined their city by attempting to conduct war by debate in the market place. Like the French Republic, they put their unsuccessful commanders to death. They treated their dependencies with such injustice that they lost their maritime empire. They plundered the rich until the rich conspired with the public enemy and they crowned their guilt by the martyrdom of Socrates.

"When the absolute sway of numbers had endured for near a quarter of a century, nothing but bare existence was left for the State to lose; and the Athenians, wearied and despondent, confessed the true cause of their ruin. . . . The

repentance of the Athenians came too late to save
the Republic.   But the lesson of their experience
endures for all times, for it teaches that government by the whole people, being the government of
the most numerous and most powerful class, is an
evil of the same nature as unmixed monarchy, and
requires, for nearly the same reasons, institutions
that shall protect it against itself, and shall
uphold the permanent reign of law against arbitrary revolutions of opinion."

The result in the Roman Republic for similar
reasons was the same.

The question which is really at issue in the
adoption of the initiative and the referendum is
whether we shall abolish constitutions, shall abolish
the standard of individual rights and shall justify
the action of the majority of an electorate which
is a minority of all the people as necessarily the
only guide to right and justice.   When it becomes
apparent, as it undoubtedly will later, what the
real meaning of this issue is, as I have stated it,
I doubt not that the American people will end this
movement, formidable and popular as it now
seems, and reverse their present tendency.   It is
said that this can not be; that the people have felt
the pleasure of the exercise of the power which
they have under the system and that they never

will willingly give it up again, lest they may be
obstructed and hampered by the intrigues and
corruptions of politicians. It is possible that the
people may never formally repeal provisions for
referendum, but my judgment is that the movement will come to an end by the non-use of the
referendum, as the people shall see the absurdities
into which it is likely to lead them. That the
initiative as an instrumentality in the hands of
cranks to impose unnecessary political duties upon
the whole body of the electorate will become
unpopular, it is easy to foretell. When the initiative is abolished as an institution, and the
referendum left to the option of the legislature,
with the experience that the people are likely to
go through with before this result is reached, we
can be confident that the use of the referendum
will be so infrequent as not to endanger the representative system, or to change materially its useful
character.

IV

THE INITIATIVE, THE REFERENDUM, THE RECALL

(CONTINUED)

I have pointed out in the last chapter a number of objections to the new system of direct government by a majority of those voting, who are usually a minority of the electorate, but I did not exhaust the arguments which can be urged against the proposed radical change in our form of government.

I must not fail to notice an argument against the introduction of the system into the state governments, which has been made by some very able opponents of this so-called reform, in which, however, I can not concur. Senator Bailey, on the floor of the Senate, contended that the proposed change would be a violation of the guaranty contained in Article 4, Section 4, of the Constitution, the language of which is:

"The United States shall guarantee to every state in this Union a republican form of government and shall protect each of them against invasion, and on application of the legislature, or of the executive when the legislature can not be convened, against domestic violence."

The insistence of Senator Bailey was, and of others who have supported him in that view, that the use of the expression "republican" form of government indicated the intention upon the part of the framers of the Constitution to secure in the States, by guaranty of the general Government, a representative form of popular government. He pointed out that the debates of the Constitutional Convention, so far as we can get at them, and the language of *The Federalist*, a contemporaneous comment on the Constitution before it was adopted by the people, showed conclusively that all the framers of the Constitution understood clearly the difference between a representative government and one in which the people exercised the power of government directly; that they had constantly in mind the difference between a republic under a system of representative government and a pure democracy, and that they were anxious to avoid the dangers which in their judgment would flow from a pure democracy.

A number of times Madison gave his definition of republicanism, and he described it as a popular representative government. In Chapter 10 of *The Federalist*, which Madison wrote, he pointed out the dangers of faction in a popular government, and then he said:

"If a faction consists of less than a majority, relief is supplied by the republican principle, which enables the majority to defeat its sinister views, by regular vote. It may clog the administration, it may convulse society; but it will be unable to execute and mask its violence under the forms of the constitution. When a majority is included in a faction, the form of popular government, on the other hand, enables it to sacrifice to its ruling passion or interest, both the public good and the rights of other citizens. To secure the public good, and private rights, against the danger of such a faction, and at the same time to preserve the spirit and the form of popular government, is then the great object to which our inquiries are directed. Let me add, that it is the great desideratum, by which alone this form of government can be rescued from the opprobrium under which it has so long laboured, and be recommended to the esteem and adoption of mankind.

"By what means is this object attainable? Evidently by one of two only. Either the existence of the same passion or interest in a majority at the same time must be prevented; or the majority having such co-existent passion or interest, must be rendered, by their number and local situation, unable to concert and carry into effect schemes of oppression. If the impulse and the opportunity be suffered to coincide, we well know, that neither moral nor religious motives can be relied on as an adequate control. They are not found to be such on the injustice and violence of individuals, and lose their efficacy in proportion to the number combined together; that is, in proportion as their efficacy becomes needful."

What does Madison mean by faction here? It is clear that he means that spirit either of a majority or minority of the electorate when it allows its action to be controlled by passion, selfish desire for its own benefit even through unjust treatment of others, and by absence of responsibility in the use of political power.

With this suggestion, let us follow Mr. Madison further in his discussion. He continues:

"From this view of the subject, it may be concluded, that a pure democracy, by which I mean a society consisting of a small number of citizens, who assemble and administer the government in person, can admit of no cure from the mischiefs of faction. A common passion or interest will, in almost every case, be felt by a majority of the whole; a communication and concert results from

the form of government itself; and there is
nothing to check the inducements to sacrifice the
weaker party, or an obnoxious individual. Hence
it is, that such democracies have ever been spec-
tacles of turbulence and contention; have ever
been found incompatible with personal security,
or the rights of property; and have, in general,
been as short in their lives, as they have been
violent in their deaths. Theoretic politicians, who
have patronized this species of government, have
erroneously supposed, that by reducing mankind
to a perfect equality in their political rights, they
would, at the same time, be perfectly equalized and
assimilated in their possessions, their opinions and
their passions.

"A republic, by which I mean a government in
which the scheme of representation takes place,
opens a different prospect, and promises the cure
for which we are seeking. Let us examine the
points in which it varies from pure democracy, and
we shall comprehend both the nature of the cure
and the efficacy which it must derive from the
union.

"The two great points of difference between a
democracy and a republic, are, first, the delega-
tion of the government, in the latter, to a small
number of citizens elected by the rest; secondly,
the greater number of citizens, and greater sphere

of country, over which the latter may be extended."

I have read this passage from Madison not only to show that he, as one of the leading spirits of the Constitutional Convention, and, therefore, probably all the others, were advised of the distinction between a republic and a pure democracy, but also to enforce the arguments of my last lecture as to the danger of direct government of a majority or a minority of the electorate, without any restraint as to the rights of the rest of the people and of individuals. But its real relevancy at this point is with reference to its bearing upon the meaning of the word "republican" used in the Constitution to support the argument of Senator Bailey and others, to which I have already referred. To Senator Bailey's argument that provision for legislation by referendum in a State government destroys its republican form, there are, it seems to me, two conclusive answers. One is that the use of the word "republican" at this point in the Constitution was not by way of contrast to a pure democracy as Madison used it in the passage quoted, or by way of emphasis upon the distinction between the two, but that it was used to describe generally the character of the governments which the embryo States had, at the

time the Constitution was being formed, and that
the contrast intended to be emphasized by this language was the contrast between a republican form
of government and a monarchical form of government, a government in which the people had control, and in which they did not have control; and
this clause was a guaranty by the National Government that every State should have a form of
government which rested upon the will of the people.   The second answer to the argument is that
the question of what is a republican form of government in this clause is a question which was
evidently committed to the discretion of Congress
ultimately to decide, because under the form
of the article the guaranty is by the general
Government, and that guaranty the general
Government must necessarily enforce, if it is to
be enforced.   The method to be pursued by the
general Government in the enforcement of such a
guaranty is by legislative and executive action,
and this necessarily relegates to Congress and the
Executive the power, political in its nature, to
determine when a State government is republican
within the meaning of this article.   To such a decision the judicial branch of the Government must
necessarily bow and can exercise no jurisdiction in
enforcement of the guaranty.   One of the most
frequent questions which Congress has been called

upon to decide is whether the constitution of an embryo state (that is a territory asking Congress for admission into the Union and tendering a constitution) secures to the State a republican form of government. Congress has acted a number of times in respect to this matter so as to leave no doubt as to the decision by this competent authority that a republican form of government guaranteed to each State by the Constitution is not limited to one which is strictly representative and may extend to one in which, by provisions for the initiative and referendum, there is an assimilation to the pure democracy and direct government.

In the case of Pacific States . . . Co. vs. the State of Oregon, 223, U. S. 118, the Supreme Court was called upon to consider the defense made by a defendant telephone company against the collection of a tax, that the tax was invalid because authority was found for it in a statute enacted into law directly by the people under the procedure by initiative and referendum, and that the statute by virtue of Section 4, Article 4, was the act of a State not having a republican form of government and was void. The Court, speaking by Chief Justice White, held that the question whether Oregon had a republican form of government was political, and was for the judgment of Congress, and that until Congress acted upon any

change in the government of Oregon, and declared
it to be a violation of the Constitution, the Court
would accept its status as determined by Congress
when it admitted Oregon into the Union.

In passing, it may be useful to call particular
attention to the action of the Supreme Court in
declining to decide this purely political question
and in remitting it to the political branch of
Government as represented by the legislature.
The Supreme Court has been attacked vigorously
in this recent and current agitation as an arbitrary repository of political power, legislative in
its character and prejudiced in its exercise, this
for the purpose of laying the foundation for the
abolition of the constitutional restraints and the
remission to the result of a popular referendum
the question of the validity of a legislative act
rather than to the decision of a court. Not only
in this case but in a great many other cases arising under the Constitution, the Supreme Court
has refused to assume power to differ with the
political branches of the government in the decision of political questions.

Recall

In coming to the question of recall, we are
brought to the consideration of something said

to be new in the instrumentalities of government, although the Athenians certainly exercised it in effect. The initiative and the referendum were inventions of the Swiss, and had been put into operation for a number of years before their adoption here, but the Swiss never had the recall. The recall is part and parcel of the plan of direct government by the people acting at once, and, as the Latin phrase has it, *dum fervet opus*, i.e., "while the issue is raging" (to give it a free translation). It is a part of what has not infrequently been called the "hair trigger" form of government, by which, immediately upon the presentation of an issue, it shall be passed upon by the electorate. The recall is an institution under which, by the petition of a certain percentage of registered voters, the question whether any elected officer shall continue in office during the term for which he was elected shall be submitted to the electors, with the feature added that any other aspirant to the office, having complied with certain formal preliminaries, may become a candidate against him in the same election in which his qualifications for office are to be reconsidered by the people. The opportunity is given in the petition for a statement of the reasons why the officer against whom the petition is filed ought to be recalled, and generally in some form or other an opportunity is given to the incumbent to state a short answer to the charges made.

It seems to me that the arguments against this method of changing the popular agents are as strong as those against the initiative and the referendum. The useful part of the plan can all be accomplished by a provision that if the officer has neglected his duty, or is guilty of malfeasance, he may be removed after a hearing by a court or by the Chief Executive. This could be made as expeditious as a fair hearing would permit and need not drag through all the courts with the officer still holding his office, but the action of the first tribunal, whether judicial or executive, could oust him, and an appeal, if taken, need not suspend the effect of the ouster until a final reversal of the first decision.

The objection to the recall is not at all the injustice to the officer in taking away from him that which the people had given him. We have lost the idea in this country that an office is the property of the officer, and such a provision as recall does not, therefore, in any way interfere with a vested right. | His comfort or enjoyment does not figure in the matter at all. The objection to the recall is its injury to efficient government and the possibility that an honest and effective official may be prevented from doing his duty by the use of such an instrument in the hands of malignant enemies, or aspiring rivals who seize the opportunity of a momentary unpopularity to deprive the public of a useful public servant. It takes away the probability of independence and courage of official action in the servants of the people. It tends to produce in every public official a nervous condition of irresolution as to whether he should do what he thinks he ought to do in the interest of the public, or should withhold from doing anything, or should do as little as possible, in order to avoid any discussion at all.

What do we have government for? It is not merely for the purpose of elections. It is not merely for the purpose of inviting the people constantly to express their opinion on issues just as an amusement. We have government for the purpose of accomplishing something, of doing something for the benefit of the people, of achieving the greatest good to the greatest number, and preserving to the individual his happiness and progress. Now I submit it is not to contribute to that end to have mere puppets in office who can not enter upon proper public policies and carry them out, because they fear that their purpose will be misunderstood before their patriotic and public objects are accomplished.

If we have the recall in the case of local officers,

there is not any logical reason why we should not have the recall in the case of all officers, and therefore that whenever proper preliminaries are established, we should have the recall of Presidents. Look back, my friends, through the history of the United States and recount the number of instances of men who filled important offices and whose greatness is conceded to-day, and tell me one who was not subject of the severest censure for what he had done, whose motives were not questioned, whose character was not attacked, and who, if subjected to a recall at certain times in his official career when criticism had impaired his popularity, would not have been sent into private life with only a part of his term completed. Washington is one who would have been recalled, Madison another, Lincoln another and Cleveland another. These were the highest types of patriots and statesmen, who adhered to a conscientious sense of duty to the public. They are men for whom to-day the verdict of history is, "Well done, thou good and faithful servant" and this, too, in respect of the very matters that at the time had subjected them to the doubt and suspicion and antagonism of a temporary majority of the people. Indeed the recall is nothing but the logical outcome of the proposition embodied in the referendum and the initiative, to wit, that government must follow the course of popular passion and momentary expression of the people without deliberation and without opportunity for full information. I am now referring to the recall of executive officers and legislative representatives, and what I have said is applicable to them. I am not now dealing with the judicial officer and the recall of the judge. That is associated with another proposition known as the recall of judicial decisions, and I shall later consider those two propositions together under another clause of the preamble.

The adoption of the initiative, referendum and recall, and the change of the character of our Government which they will involve, is but flying in the face of the indisputable verdict of history, and the plainest inference that the logic of circumstances can enforce. These "hair trigger" popular verdicts are said to be progressive, and to be the means of a growth toward better things. They are advocated as necessary steps in advancing civilization. The facts contradict altogether such a view. It is a case of atavism. It is adopting a theory of government that was rejected thousands of years ago because of its utter failure to survive the inherent difficulties presented in its practical operation.

I would not minimize in the slightest degree the

advantage that will doubtless arise in our Government from the stimulated interest of the people in stamping out certain evils of our political system to which I have referred. Those evils were largely possible because of the lack of that popular attention which is now being more or less roused to the consideration of our Government, our social condition and those inequalities of opportunity and condition which it is wise for our Government to attempt to modify and remedy. But the warning in which all practical and patriotic men must join is that these so-called novel methods, approval of which is now made a test of the real progressive spirit, mean only a reversion to a type that has been proven to be a failure and will necessarily lead to a defeat of all the good purposes and real benefits of popular government. Unrestrained tyranny of the majority will lead to anarchy, and anarchy will lead the people to embrace and support the absolute rule of one rather than the turbulent and unreasonable whim of a factional majority.

Of course, I understand the penalty that one has to undergo in taking this position, of being charged with prejudice in favor of special interests, and against popular government, and with failing to recognize the great change which has come over the people. The leaders of the movement dwell upon the regeneration of the political character of the people, and their really religious enthusiasm and the growth of self-abnegation among them. Therefore, it is said that we must not look to the past as an evidence or a proof of what will happen by the introduction of these old methods.

I had the pleasure of listening to a sermon in New York preceding the last election, in which it was pointed out that, except in respect of the slavery issue, politics in America had since the foundation of the Government been commercial, sordid and concerned with the material side of life, but that from this time on the issues were not to be merely commercial and economical, but were to present the higher aspirations on the one side, and a retrogression on the other, and that all that was necessary was for the people to choose; that we had escaped from the dominion of the slavish accumulators of wealth, and that we were now moving on to a higher level and to the cultivation of the pure brotherhood of man. This view was not very complimentary to the great men that established this government, or the patriots and statesmen who have figured since in American history, and it struck me as unduly optimistic. No one should hold in contempt the aspiration for better things nor employ ridicule to confute argument based upon it, but the plain facts can not be destroyed by mere eloquence.

The character of the people is made up by the character of the individuals that compose it. The truth is that the conscience of the crowd is never as sensitive, and never represents as high ideals, as the conscience of the individual, and the soundness of the view that the people are now ready for a form of government which, in the past, they have not been able to exercise with any utility to themselves, must rest upon our knowledge of the individual. I would not deny at all that there are enthusiasts who conscientiously feel the spur of brotherly love and of anxiety to bring about a condition in which that sentiment shall be embodied in our statutes and in our governmental policies, and in all relations in life between individuals, and that there are those who are willing to make real sacrifices to bring about such a state, even to the giving up of the advantages of comfort and wealth and position that they now enjoy in society. But has sin left us? Has the principle of enlightened or other kind of selfishness ceased to operate on the individual? Are we not all subject to the weaknesses of human nature that we have known for six thousand years? And do those weaknesses not manifest themselves in elections as well as in other phases of individual duty? Is it the wise part of statesmanship to ignore these truths and the character of the individual and of the people as we know them to-day, and proceed to adopt a form of government on the theory that they have entirely changed, and that each man bears to the other a feeling of altruism and of brotherly love that will make him ignore his own condition and look after his brother's only? We know this is not so. Though we accept the proposition that the people have grown more sensitive than they were when they permitted corruption and corrupt control of state legislatures and other instrumentalities of government by their inertia and their failure to act, must we not admit that in the States where the new direct system has been introduced, we find a majority of the voters neglecting their public duties so that measures are being adopted by a comparatively small minority, and not by the majority?

This movement back of the referendum, initiative and recall does not find its only promptings in a desire to stamp out corruption. There is another basis for the movement to-day which gives strength to the proposal to put unrestrained and immediate control in the hands of a majority or minority of the electorate. It is in the idea that the unrestrained rule of the majority of the electors voting will prevent the right of property

from proving an obstacle to achieving equality in
condition so that the rich may be made poorer and
the poor richer. In other words, a spur, con-
scious or unconscious, to this movement is socialistic. It may not be recognized, even by those who
are acting under its influence, but it is there, and
ultimately it will manifest itself so plainly that
no one can be blinded as to its real meaning and
purpose.

I can not at this time consider properly the
wisdom and soundness of the doctrine that lies at
the basis of socialism, or put a true and full estimate upon the value of the preservation of the
right of property in our political, governmental
and economic systems. Nor do I impeach the
good faith or intentions of socialists. It is sufficient for me now to say that next to the right of
liberty, the right of property is the most important individual right guaranteed by the Constitution and the one which, united with that of
personal liberty, has contributed more to the
growth of civilization than any other institution
established by the human race. If it is to be elimi-
nated from the rights secured to the individual,
then we shall see disappear from our community
the mainspring of action that has led men to labor,
to save, to invent, to devise plans for making two
blades of grass grow where one grew before, to

increase the production of all human comforts and to reduce their cost; we shall see a halt in thrift, providence, industry, mental and physical activity and energy because they will no longer command the rewards that have heretofore stimulated them, and society will sink to a dead level of those who will seek to get along with the least labor, least effort and least self-sacrifice. Socialism proposes no adequate substitute for the motive of enlightened selfishness that to-day is at the basis of all human labor and effort, enterprise and new activity.

There is reason to believe that the tendency of much of what has been termed "unrest" in society has been fed and stimulated by the jealousy of those who with envious eye are now looking upon the rewards of thrift and saving and enterprise enjoyed by others. Then, too, these proposed radical changes in our political and social structure have found ready support from those sincere lovers of their kind whose judgment has been led astray by a constant contemplation of the suffering and misfortune in the world, and whose sense of the due proportion of things has thus been affected so that they can not see the real progress that has been made in the comfort and enjoyment and opportunity of the average individual to-day over that which the average individual enjoyed fifty, one hundred or two hundred years ago.

Do we find in the propaganda of this modern school of thinkers who are engaged in organizing the new millennium, any appeal for industry, thrift and the discharge of duty by all the people? Is not the picture constantly held out to the people that they are the victims of a conspiracy against them by those who appear to be the more fortunate? Is there not in every line of the addresses and the speeches and the platforms that are issued to arouse the people, the assumption that they have discharged their duty in every regard? Are not those who achieve under modern conditions the greater comfort by hard work and prudential virtues held up as in some way to blame for the fact that those who are not so thrifty, and who have not labored with the same assiduity and with the same self-sacrifice do not have the same comforts?

I would not minimize the number of the unfortunate who in the struggle for existence have fallen behind through the hardness of conditions rather than through their lack of industry and thrift. Wherever the present law by reason of its ancient derivation fails to square with the just requirements of modern conditions, I would amend it, and one good thing that this present movement

is accomplishing is the modification of the harder
and narrower provisions of the common law so as
to put the employees of little power and means on
a level with their employers in adjusting and
agreeing upon their mutual obligations. Indeed,
no objection exists to the proposal to introduce
what is called "collectivist" legislation, if sensibly
and practically conceived, in which the rights of
classes against each other may be recognized, and
the classes placed on such an equality as to
opportunity as the law can properly effect. But
it is a real injury to society to emphasize constantly the necessity for ameliorating the conditions of the less fortunate and the people of little
means, without at the same time dwelling upon
their duties as citizens, their obligation to render
a full day's work for a full day's wages, their
duty to sympathize with the enforcement of law
and to render justice even to the more fortunate
members of the community. Instead of this,
appeals are really being made to the majority to
use the power that their being a majority gives
them to compel equality, not only of opportunity
but of condition and of property, and, by silence
on the subject, to ignore all difference in point of
merit between thrift and industry on the one hand,
and shiftlessness and laziness on the other.

Let the movement in favor of purer and better

government go on. Let it disclose itself in the
effective attention to the election of our representatives in executive and legislative offices, and to
the holding of them to strict responsibility. But
let us not, with a confession that we, the people, are
incapable of selecting honest representatives,
assume the still more difficult office and duty of
directly discharging the delicate functions of
government by the hasty action of a necessarily
uninformed majority of the electorate, or, what is
more likely, by a minority of an electorate, a
majority of which declines to take part in the
government through disgust at the impracticable
and unwise burdens that are sought to be thrown
upon them.

I have no doubt that this movement toward
direct government, or, as it is called, toward pure
democracy, with a view of giving absolute power
to a majority of the voting class, will continue for
some time to come. I am not blind at all to the
strength of the movement for the initiative,
referendum and recall. I am quite aware that I
am swimming against the stream but this does not
discourage me or make my conviction less strong.
The impatience at constitutional restraints will
grow with the longing for absolute power by the
voting minority. But I am very hopeful that
when the American people, after many humiliat-

ing experiences and difficulties of their own making, shall see that the ultimate issue is socialism
and an unlimited control of the majority of the
electorate on the one hand, or our present government on the other, they will make the wise choice
and will give up this new solution of the problems
of society. They will then return to an appreciation of the wisdom of our ancestors in the framing
of a government of the people, for the people, by
the people, in which the checks and balances
secure deliberation and wisdom in ultimate popular action, and protect the individual in the
enjoyment of those rights which have enabled him
and his fellows to carry society and civilization
to the high point which they have reached in the
history of human kind.

As Mr. Lincoln said in his first inaugural:

"A majority held in restraint by constitutional
checks and limitations and always changing easily
with deliberate changes of popular opinion and
sentiment is the only true sovereign of the people.
Whoever rejects it, does of necessity fly to
anarchy or despotism."

V

The Direct Primary

In the discussion of the expression, "We, the people," set forth in the preamble of the Constitution, my remarks have taken the wide range of a consideration of the electorate, and the methods and procedure adopted for securing an expression of the will of the people, and the proper limitations and restraints in such procedure for the purpose of securing deliberation and the clear exercise of popular judgment after full information.

There is one other proposed reform that has been associated with the new methods of initiative, referendum and recall, though not necessarily involving them or involved in them. I mean the direct primary. That is a method of selecting the party candidates to be voted for in the election by a preliminary election of the members of the party. It is also usual and necessary to have a declaration of party principles so that the whole electorate may know what may be expected if the party succeeds in electing its candidates and controls the legislature and the executive. The direct primary itself can not furnish this, and it is usually accompanied by some plan for securing such a declaration either from a party committee or a conference of candidates. The same evils which have prompted a resort to such radical methods as the initiative, the referendum and the recall, have also stimulated a wish to change the old methods of party government, of the selection of party candidates, and the declaration of party principles.

In many States until a few years ago the controlling element in a party was practically self-perpetuating. The qualifications of those whose votes or preferences were allowed to control the selection of the local committees and managers of the party, were so limited that it was an easy matter for the leaders of the party to continue their power. They became properly known as the bosses of a machine. The machine strengthened itself whenever the party was successful by distributing the patronage thus secured to create an organization of office-holders, or expectant office-holders, which was well-nigh invincible in the party councils and in determining party policy.

Of course, the managers of great corporations that entered into politics for the purpose of preventing raids upon them, or for the purpose of securing undue privilege from the public, found

such machines and organizations ready tools for
their hands to attain their purposes, and with the
corruption fund which they were able to take from
their profits, they supplemented the use of patronage to lubricate the machine and make it operate
with certain efficiency for the achievement of their
ends. When the people were aroused to the sense
of their danger from corrupt corporate control
in the government, they properly turned to the
boss system and the political machine as the
instrument which enabled the powers of evil and
of corruption to control parties, and through
parties to control governments. They, therefore,
directed their energies toward legislation which
would take away the means of support upon which
bosses and machines had thrived. They found
that the local political conventions and the cau-
cuses of a limited membership which did not by
any means admit or include the whole electorate
of the party, selected the delegates to the local
municipal, county and district conventions in
which were nominated the municipal officers and
the representatives to the State legislature and
the members of Congress. In the same conventions were elected the delegates to the State conventions, which in turn selected the Governor and
the other officers of state. Each caucus and each
convention gave opportunity for manipulation by

the machine, so that the real rank and file of the party except the comparatively few "insiders" had little voice in the preliminary selecting of candidates and declaring of party principles. The only modification of this absolute power which the machine maintained was through the vote of the people at the election upon the result of the machine's work. The healthy fear of a defeat at the polls frequently led to the nomination for those offices, which did not give the incumbents great political power, of good candidates in order to attract the support of the party and the independent voter. For offices of patronage and political power the agents of the machine were generally nominated.

I may stop a little to refer to this influence which we call the force of public opinion. It is the saving grace in the defects of popular government. It grows out of publicity and a free press. It is what has made government in communities possible and even tolerable under conditions that when stated seem necessarily to involve the most revolting and demoralizing corruption and tyrannical boss rule. It is what has enabled the great municipal community of New York City, the greatest city in this country and one of the greatest in the world, to live under such a control as that of Tammany and still have a useful government, effective in many ways, though with many faults. This public opinion is made up not by the views of the electorate alone, but by those of the whole people, including women, minors and residents ineligible to vote, reflected in the press and reaching those in power in a thousand different ways. It exists, of course, to some extent in every form of government, however tyrannical, but it has its full flower among an intelligent, active and enterprising people who support a free, courageous, alert and discriminating press, the individual members of which present different aspects of the facts and of the issues, but which united together present in composite form an evidence of the public will that places a most healthy restraint upon the otherwise irresponsible boss or machine manager. The distinction between a people capable of self-government and one that should be still in leading strings is shown more in the difference in the intelligence and effective power of public opinion of the two peoples than in any other way. I remember an incident in the Philippine Islands when I was Governor that made me dwell upon such a difference. I was waited on by a committee of respectable Filipino gentlemen, who asked permission to form and exploit a political party for the securing of independence by peaceable means. I told them they could do so without securing my permission, but I cautioned them that, as there were men then engaged in active and open revolt against the government, the organization and maintenance of such a party, before peace was restored, might subject them to annoying curiosity and suspicion of government agents and officers. They said that they and their people were used to securing direct authority from the Governor-General in Spanish times for such a political movement and they did not wish to go into it unless I approved. They wished, therefore, to satisfy me that the Filipinos were capable of self-government, and they could do so in a paper they would leave me. The argument presented was based on the statistics as to education in the Islands and the number of offices to be filled in the central, provincial and municipal government. As these showed that there were twice as many educated people as there were offices, they considered their case established, because it gave the people of the Philippines the benefit of two shifts of public servants, and a people would be unreasonable that wanted more. I attempted to explain to them that it was the average intelligence of the whole people that constituted their governmental capacity, and this not only because a considerable part of them took part in elections, but because of this force of public

opinion coming from the whole people and re-
straining public servants in every conceivable way.
I don't think I convinced my petitioners but it
made me formulate for my own benefit and future
use a statement of that great saving force in a
government of a free and intelligent people.

But to return to the party primary. A party
is a voluntary organization, and originally the
natural theory was that the members of the party
should be left to themselves to determine how their
party representatives .were to be selected and
their party principles were to be formulated; but
the abuses to which completely voluntary organizations of this kind led, brought about a change of
view as to the function of the government with
reference to such party procedure.

The first step taken was to provide legal machinery and regulations for the holding of party
primaries and a convention in the local divisions,
which the party authorities might by proper legal
notice make applicable to the selection of their
candidates and the declaration of their principles
before any election. It was voluntary. It was
left to the committees of the parties to indicate
their wish to act under the law by formal notice,
and then it became binding, and penalties followed
the breach of its provisions as declared in the
law.

This legislation, however, did not prove to be enough, and so those who wished to bring about honest methods in politics determined to make a compulsory law for the government of parties who ·proposed to present candidates at any election. Parties thus came to be recognized as official entities and the laws for the holding of primaries and of conventions have become as specific in their provisions and as severe in their penalties for violations as the election law itself. The officers who are appointed as judges and clerks of regular elections are made to discharge similar functions in party primary elections, and the State bears the expense, on the theory that the whole public are interested, that each party should honestly select its candidates and declare its principles.

I fully concur in the critical importance that this character of legislation attaches to party action, and I do not hesitate to say that we have not yet arrived at a satisfactory solution of the problem presented.

It must be obvious to every one that while all members of the party who can vote ought to have a voice in the selection of candidates and in the determination of principles, it is in the highest degree unfair for persons who are not members of the party, but members of some other party, to exercise any influence in the selection of the candidates or the declaring of the principles. So the most difficult question in all primary laws is the one which confronts the reforming legislator on the threshold. It is how to determine properly and certainly who are qualified electors at a party primary. The other question, which is its counterpart, is to discover who are not entitled to vote, so that if they do vote, they shall be punished and sent to prison for their violation of law and justice. Shall the party electorate be limited to those who are willing to swear that they voted for the party candidates who ran in the last election? Must they have voted for all the candidates? Would not a vote for a majority of the candidates entitle the voter to stand as a regular party man and to vote at the party primary? Or must the qualifications be determined not by what the voter has done in the past, but by what he intends to do in the future? Shall it be enough for him to say that he intends to vote for the party candidates and to follow what he understands to be the party's principles in the next election? The advantage of having the qualifications fixed by what the voter has done in the past is that the definite issue of his qualification then presented is dependent upon an ascertainable fact. If he has not voted as he says he has voted, then he is guilty of perjury and guilty of a plain attempt to defeat the law and secure a vote which is illegal. Prosecutions for frauds of this character would soon keep voters in primaries of their own party.

On the other hand, it is urged that if men have conscientiously reached the conclusion that they intend to be Republicans or Democrats thereafter, it would seem that they ought to have a right to partake in the selection of the candidates to represent them. But the objection to this is that when it comes to an oath as to what they are going to do, there is no means of determining, except in the mind of the man who is taking the oath, what the fact is. He is swearing as to a mental state, and he is the best witness of that state, and nobody can contradict him in any such way as to subject him to conviction for perjury, even if he never intended to support the party. The fact that he subsequently actually votes for some other candidate in the election than the candidate of the party in whose primary he has cast a vote, is not clinching evidence of the fraud he has committed, because he can say he changed his mind and he can hardly be contradicted.

The evil that has proceeded from this uncertainty as to the qualifications of party electors has become so great that I venture to think that the wiser and more practical rule will be to limit party electors for the purpose of selecting candidates in the future to those who supported the party at the last election. That is always or generally a large enough body to secure a disinterested vote, or at least secure a vote that is not under the control of any machine or any pernicious influence.

The reports leave no doubt whatever, indeed the statistics of the elections frequently conclusively confirm the conclusion, that in State and other primaries, thousands and tens of thousands of Democrats vote at Republican primaries, and vice versa. It often happens that in one party, a primary issue, like the selection of a candidate, is settled in advance by general agreement as to who the candidate shall be or what the principle shall be. In such a case the voters of that party feel entirely free to go into the primaries of the other party, and sometimes, with malice aforethought, to vote for the candidate in that party whom it will be most easy for the candidate of their own party to defeat at the general election.

Of course this is all wrong. This is not taking the voice of the party. It is taking the voice of men who are not interested that the party should succeed, and who do not intend to be genuine supporters of the men whom they put upon the party ticket.

In connection with this subject, I am reminded

of an experience I had in local politics in Cincinnati, my home. Soon after I came to the Bar, I was living in the 5th Ward, which in those days included within its boundaries both a well-to-do quarter and one which was not. Our precinct had frequently been represented in local Republican conventions by a man named Martin Muldoon, who was reported to have made a modest competence in this service. Living in the same precinct with me was another reformer named Aaron Ferris. He had a most solemn countenance and a voice and bearing of the most monitory and minatory kind. He was a perfect Puritan in type. We agreed that something ought to be done to oust Martin from his representative functions. Accordingly we drummed up as many Republican voters as we could through the precinct and urged them to be alive to their political duties and attend the primary. But we found that we were likely to be swamped by many Democrats who had always voted for Martin in a Republican primary in honorable return for aid which Martin and his Republican voters gave some candidate of theirs in a Democratic primary. It was agreed that we could only escape this result by securing one of the judges and by energy in challenging. Ferris' qualifications fitted him exactly for the judgeship and my then somewhat formidable proportions seemed to make it appropriate for me to take the office of outside challenger. The plan was put through without awaking the suspicions of Martin to the extent of installing Ferris as judge. The first man who came to the polls was Michael Flannigan. I nearly created a riot by challenging his vote. Michael's attitude was that of indignant surprise and offended dignity, and his aspect became threatening, but I persisted in my challenge and stated as a ground that he was a Democrat and not entitled to vote in a Republican primary. Then was vindicated our choice of Ferris as a judge. Minos of Crete could not have seemed more forbidding as he produced a Bible and demanded, in deep tones, of the would-be voter that before he give true reply to the questions he was about to ask him, he should place his hand upon the Book, and repeat after him: "I solemnly swear, in the presence of Almighty God, as I shall answer at the last day of Judgment, that I am Republican"—Ferris had not gone further when Flannigan jerked his hand away, retreated from the poll, muttering "To h—l with the vote." The effect was instantaneous and work as Martin would, he could bring only a few who would or could pass the examination. We had rallied enough of our own side to defeat Martin under these conditions and we sent a good man to act as delegate. But Martin advised me then that that would be the last time Aaron Ferris would be permitted to be a judge at a primary election in that precinct.

This story illustrates the difficulty in holding fair primaries, but I agree it does not suggest a means of avoiding it that would always succeed. Ferrises are not always to be had as judges and would-be voters are not always as afraid of an oath, however solemn.

It seems to have been the opinion in the Courts of some States that in carrying on an election of this sort, no citizen, whatever his party, could be deprived of the right to vote in either primary. Such a construction may turn upon peculiar language in a state constitution, but the result is so absurd in the provision for a party primary that it can not for a moment be sustained on general principles and is utterly at war with fairness and honesty in party control.

Until some method has been devised successfully to prevent this fraud I have been describing, we can not be said to have a successful primary law. Of course, it is helpful to have party primaries of all parties on the same day. In this way, if there is a real controversy in all parties, the voters are likely to divide themselves according to their real and sincere party affiliations, because one can only

vote in one primary; but the case of a lively fight
in one party and none in another is so frequent
that the difficulty I have suggested is often a
real one.

The first impulse, and a proper one, of the
honest legislator, in dealing with this subject, is
to give all the members of the party an equal
voice in the selection of candidates and in the
declaration of party principles. Therefore all
the rules which limit the caucus to the active few,
or which exclude regular members of the party,
have been properly abolished under such primary
statutes, and provision is made for every such
member to cast his ballot.

The question upon which opinions differ vitally
is whether these electors of the party shall cast
their ballots directly for their candidates to be run
at the general election, or whether they shall select
delegates to local conventions, the candidates to
be selected in the local conventions. The modern
tendency is toward the direct selection of candidates by the party electors themselves, without the
intervention of a convention. I am inclined to
think that for a time at least this elimination of
the party convention in local politics is a good
thing.

Theoretically the convention would be better
for reasons which can be very shortly stated. If

all the electors, divided into wards and precincts, could select honest and intelligent delegates to represent them in a convention, and these delegates were to give their best thought and disinterested effort to the selection of candidates, I have no doubt that the candidates selected would be better for the party and better for the people than the candidates selected directly at a primary. And this is because the delegates can better inform themselves as to the qualifications of the party candidates than can the people at large. And, secondly, the delegates of a party have a sense of responsibility in selecting the party candidates to secure the support of the people at the general election which is utterly absent in the votes which are cast by the electors of the party at the direct primary polls. There the party electors vote for the men who have been brought favorably to their attention by the newspapers and other means of publicity which the candidates themselves are able to adopt and use. They cast their votes very much as the electors at a general election cast their votes, for the men whom they like, or the men whom they know, and frequently without much knowledge or preference at all. Whereas, in a convention, the leaders and the delegates have the keenest care with respect to what is going to happen at the general election.

In the selection of State and national candidates, this becomes a very important matter. One tendency in a direct election of candidates in a national party will be to select a popular partisan, while that of a convention system will be to take the more moderate man whose name will appeal to the independent voter. Thus a primary election in 1860 would certainly have nominated Seward, not Lincoln; in 1876 would have nominated Blaine, not Hayes.

A third objection to the direct election of candidates by the people is the obvious advantage which the men with wealth and of activity and of little modesty, but of great ambition to be candidates, without real qualification for office, have over the men who, having qualifications for office, are either without means or refuse to spend money for such a purpose, and are indisposed to press their own fitness upon the voters. In other words, the direct election of candidates very much reduces the probability that the office will seek the man.

Whenever I hear or see the phrase "the office seeking the man," I am reminded of a story I have frequently told, that I heard when I was on the Federal Bench and holding court in Kentucky. A Republican Governor had been selected for the first time in the history of the State. An old man, named Aleck Carter, from one of the mountain counties of the State, where live the great majority of such Republicans as there are in Kentucky, who had been voting the Republican ticket all his life, and apparently to no purpose, journeyed down on an old mare from the mountains to Frankfort, the capital. The Kingdom had come and he wished to be there to see, and also to get his reward. When he applied for an office, he was told that in contrast to Democratic methods, this was to be an administration in which the spirit of reform was strong and that the office was to seek the man. He put up at the Capitol Hotel for ten days; then he changed to a boarding house, and finally he merely hired a room and relied on his friends and free lunches for sustenance. But the hour came when neither money nor credit nor Kentucky hospitality could tide him over another day and he must go. As he went by the Capitol Hotel, where the politicians were gathered, an acquaintance called out to him: "Aleck, where are you going?" "I am going home," said he. "I've heard tell, since I've been here, a good mite about an office seeking a man, but I hain't met any office of that kind. My money's gin out and I'm bound for the mountains." Then a hopeful thought seemed to strike him and he continued, "But if any of 'youuns' see

an office hunting a man, tell 'em that you just seen
Aleck Carter on his old mare 'Jinny' going down
the Versailles pike and he was going damn slow."

Were Aleck yearning for an office under the
dispensation of direct primaries, he would not be
embarrassed by any such newfangled fashion in
official preferment, for it has no vogue in the days
of the direct primary.

The direct primary puts a premium on self-
seeking of an office. After men are nominated as
party candidates, the party is behind them, and
can elect them even though they modestly refrain
from exploiting themselves. But in the stage
previous to this, when the candidates are to be
selected at a direct primary for a party, modest
but qualified men are never selected. This sub-
stantially lessens the number of available candidates capable by reason of their intelligence and
experience of filling the offices well.

I have thus stated three serious objections to
the direct election of candidates by the people
for local offices and for representatives in Congress and the legislature, and yet I do not think
that they are sufficient to overcome the present
necessity of avoiding the evils that have arisen
from the delegate and convention systems so far
as these local and district officers are concerned.
The delegates selected for the local convention are

many of them usually not of a character to resist the blandishments and the corrupt means which will in such cases be used by bosses and the principals of bosses. The local convention of local delegates offers such a rich opportunity for manipulation of those who are corruptible,— things are done so quickly by committees of credentials, and on resolutions,—that the opportunity of the unscrupulous boss in such a convention is very great. I sympathize, therefore, with the movement to abolish the local convention, at least until the exercise of the direct primary shall have broken up the local machines and shall have given an opportunity to the electors of the party, even with the disadvantage of inadequate information, to express their will.

When, however, the question is of the State convention and its continuance in politics, I am strongly inclined to a different opinion. The delegates who are sent to a state convention should be voted for directly by the same electorate that selects the representatives to the legislatures, and their character is likely to be very much higher than that of the delegates to a local convention. The circumstances offer as much reason for confidence in their honesty as in that of those who are selected for the legislature by the primary. The unit of a national party in a practical sense is the

State party. That is the body that helps to formulate a political policy for the national party. If the party has a majority in the legislature, it ought to have a State policy, the determination and declaration of which can best be had in a convention. It is not indispensable that the parties in local controversies should announce principles at all, and, therefore, the necessity for a local convention on that account is really small. But when it comes to a party of the State, there ought· to be some body having representative authority to declare what the party policies are to be. Now in some States there has been substituted for the party convention an assembly of party candidates, and in others of the elected party managers from each county, but none of these methods secures a reliable expression of what the party opinion really is as well as a State convention with delegates selected for the purpose.

I do not mean to say that there is not any opportunity in a State convention for political manipulation. I do not mean to say that corrupt politicians will not try to be influential, and will not succeed in some directions, as they will under any system, but I do mean to say that the opportunity for manipulation and the defeat of the will of the party electors is very much less in a state convention than it is in a local convention. It is the best means of securing an authoritative expression of the party, and offers comparatively little opportunity for boss control if the primaries at which the delegates are selected are conducted by the same method as in the direct selection of candidates for legislative representatives.

The holding of a State convention gives an opportunity for consultation among party leaders. Party leaders are not necessarily dishonest men. On the contrary, the great majority of them are honest and anxious for the party to succeed by serving the people well in the government with which the party may be entrusted. Consultation should not be tabooed. Conference and discussion lead to wise results, and conference and discussion and deliberation with reference to party policies are not possible at the polls. They are not possible when the electors number into the millions. The abolition of the State convention in my judgment, though it may be the result of the present movement, is an extreme measure which subsequent experience will show to have been a mistake.

I think it will be found—at least that has been the result of my experience in hunting for material for judicial appointments—that the method of selecting State candidates through direct vote, rather than by nomination of a convention, has not been as successful in securing as good judicial material as the old method of conventions. The result in such direct primaries is unduly affected by the fortuitous circumstance as to whose name is at the head of the list of candidates, or by the fact that he is the incumbent and his name but not his qualification is known.

The direct election of candidates for office by the people shows better results in small communities than it does with electorates like that of a state, because the character of local candidates can be very much more certainly and definitely known, and the choice made with more discrimination by the people of a local neighborhood.

What I have said with respect to a state convention applies even more forcibly to a national convention. There are public men of influence who contend that we ought to have a general national primary to settle upon candidates. I think this is carrying the direct action of the people in the selection of candidates far beyond what is practicable. The defects of the present primary system, especially that one which I have already pointed out, the impossibility of preventing voters of the opposition from voting in the party primary, would be emphasized to such a point that the selection of a candidate by popular vote would be much less satisfactory than the system of a convention attended by delegates selected by properly conducted primaries in congressional districts, or by a convention of a state. The necessity for a national convention ultimately to determine the national party policy, and to consider carefully the qualifications of candidates, I hope will always be recognized. There is not any objection—indeed there ought to be no hesitation about it—to making the representation in the convention proper and fair, so that the voters of the party may have an influence as nearly proportionate to the influence they wield in the election as is practicable. If there are rotten boroughs, as there are doubtless, under the present system, they ought to be eradicated, but to go to the other extreme of abolishing a convention which has always been the method of selecting a President, is, it seems to me, altogether unwise.

There is a tendency on the part of those who favor the direct election by the people at a party primary in all cases, to resort to loud declamation in favor of a method that gives all people their choice. I have commented on the fact that the electors are not all the people, and that others are interested in the government beside the electors; but I submit that the question is not to be governed by the general declaration that an expression of all the people at an election is necessarily better than the expression of their delegates in convention, and that the mere assertion is not proof. The real end that we have in view is a better government for each individual and for all the people, and if we can get better candidates, and if we can more surely secure the intelligent and deliberate consideration of party principle through conventions, then we should adopt conventions because what we are after is good results. The voting of all the people on an issue, or for a candidate, is not the end. It is a means, and if it is not the best means of securing good candidates and of accurately interpreting the deliberate judgment of the people, then it is not the means that ought to be adopted.

I close the discussion of this general primary, having pointed out the arguments for and against the features which are now forming the subject of discussion. While the general primary is always classed as part of the so-called reforms of the initiative, the referendum and the recall, I do not consider that they have any necessary relation. It is very essential that we should have party machinery which will prevent as far as practical corrupt bossing of the party and consequent corrupt bossing of the community, and the direct primary in local elections with certain limitations is a practical step to oust the boss and destroy the machine built of patronage and corruption. This all honest men are in favor of, if the means proposed is really effective.

We must have party government in this country. A popular government can not be made efficient without parties, and as parties now include millions of voters, it is essential that some means should be determined by which the party will can be best interpreted into the selection of candidates and the declaration of principles.

I have described the machinery of old and the machinery at present, and that which is proposed. I have attempted to point out the defects in each, and I look forward to the next ten years as probably furnishing a composite system which shall give us the best practical result. Of course, no system can avoid the effect of corruption. None can be boss or machine proof, but some method can be adopted which will minimize these evils and bring about the healthy control of party agencies by the people who compose it.

VI

"In Order to Form a More Perfect Union"

The first purpose stated in the preamble of the
Constitution for its framing and adoption was "in
order to form a more perfect union." The Articles of Confederation, under which the War of the
Revolution had been conducted, were inadequate
in many particulars. The Continental Congress
really had but little power. It conducted the war
through committees; it appointed the commanding generals, but its requisitions upon States for
money and men were nothing but recommendations, sometimes followed and sometimes ignored,
and its exercise of the function of law-making was
very limited.

The condition of the colonies after the recognition of our independence by Great Britain was
not encouraging. There was no authority anywhere sufficient to better conditions. Hamilton's
description was not an exaggeration when he
wrote in *The Federalist* in Paper XV:

"We may indeed, with propriety, be said to
have reached almost the last stage of national
humiliation. There is scarcely any thing that can
wound the pride, or degrade the character, of an

independent people, which we do not experience. Are there engagements, to the performance of which we are held by every tie respectable among men? These are the subjects of constant and unblushing violation. Do we owe debts to foreigners, and to our own citizens, contracted in a time of imminent peril, for the preservation of our political existence? These remain without any proper or satisfactory provision for their discharge. Have we valuable territories and important posts in the possession of a foreign power, which, by express stipulations, ought long since to have been surrendered? These are still retained, to the prejudice of our interest not less than of our rights. Are we in a condition to resent, or to repeal the aggression? We have neither troops, nor treasury, nor government. Are we even in a condition to remonstrate with dignity? The just imputations on our own faith, in respect to the same treaty, ought first to be removed. Are we entitled, by nature and compact, to a free participation in the navigation of the Mississippi? Spain excludes us from it. Is public credit an indispensable resource in time of public danger? We seem to have abandoned its cause as desperate and irretrievable. Is commerce of importance to national wealth? Ours is at the lowest point of declension. Is respectability in the eyes of foreign powers, a safeguard against foreign encroachments? The imbecility of our government even forbids them to treat with us. Our ambassadors abroad are the mere pageants of mimic sovereignty."

After speaking of the unnatural decrease in the value of land, and the absence of private credit, he said:

"To shorten an enumeration of particulars which can afford neither pleasure nor instruction, it may in general be demanded what indication is there of national disorder, poverty, and insignificance, that could befall a community so peculiarly blessed with natural advantages as we are, which does not form a part of the dark catalogue of our public misfortunes?"

He points out the cause as follows:

"The great and radical vice, in the construction of the existing confederation, is in the principle of legislation for states or governments, in their corporate or collective capacities, and as contradistinguished from the individuals of whom they consist."

He emphasizes the remedy in these words:

"But if we are unwilling to be placed in this perilous situation; if we still adhere to the design of a national government, or, which is the same thing, of a superintending power, under the direction of a common council, we must resolve to incorporate into our plan those ingredients, which may be considered as forming the characteristic difference between a league and a government; we must extend the authority of the union to the persons of the citizens—the only proper objects of government."

Another and very important condition in the Confederacy which created the desire for a more perfect union is stated by Madison, in the forty-second number of *The Federalist,* where he comments on the power given Congress in the proposed new constitution to regulate commerce between the States. He says:

"The defect of power in the existing confederacy, to regulate the commerce between its several members, is in the number of those which have been clearly pointed out by experience. . . . A very material object of this power was the relief of the states which import and export through other states, from the improper contributions levied on them by the latter. Were these at liberty to regulate the trade between state and state, it must be foreseen that ways would be found out to load the articles of import and export, during the passage through their jurisdiction, with duties which would fall on the makers of the latter, and the consumers of the former. We may be assured by past experience that such a practice would be introduced by future contrivances; and both by that and a common knowledge of human affairs, that it would nourish unceasing animosities and not improbably terminate in serious interruptions of the public tranquillity."

Thus we see that the use of the expression "more perfect union," if it was intended to imply that the union then existing was anything like perfect, was unjustified and inaccurate. The union was so lacking in a firm bond between its members that it really is wonderful that the fabric of a government, if it can be so called, did not come tumbling down before a change was made.

The Constitutional Convention was held behind closed doors and the several accounts of its proceedings and the debates are not complete or full. All students of the Constitution are greatly indebted to Prof. Max Farrand, of this university, for assembling the accounts into one work, where a comprehensive view of all that is known of the making of that wonderful instrument can be had, and for his excellent history on the subject.

After it was signed and reported to the Congress, Hamilton, Madison and Jay joined in the work of expounding and justifying it in *The Federalist*. There were many who opposed it with vigor, and that largely because it greatly reduced the power of the then independent States. Clinton of New York, Samuel Adams of Massachusetts, and Patrick Henry of Virginia, were among those who doubted and objected. The feeling which had roused opposition to the ratification by the States, at once upon its going into force led to a controversy over its construction, and to a movement for its amendment. Parties were formed on these issues. Mr. Jefferson and the strict constructionists who exalted the power of the States were the Republican party, which has now become the Democratic party. Hamilton, Adams, Marshall and others who favored a strong central government and a curtailing of the power of the several States, in order to make a Nation, were the Federalist party. Mr. Jefferson insisted that the Constitution did not contain a sufficient protection to the individual, and there were, therefore, proposed in Congress, at its first session, ten amendments, which were ratified on the fifth of December, 1791. The first eight of these were really a bill of rights to protect individuals against the aggression of Congress and Federal authority.

It may be as well to note at this point that the

original bill of rights of the Federal Constitution was not a restraint of the State governments against the infraction of individual rights, but a restraint of the National Government. The Fourteenth Amendment was adopted July 20, 1868. It placed in the hands of the Federal Government the enforcement of the personal rights of every person in the United States. That section provides "No state shall make or enforce any law which shall abridge the privileges or immunities of citizens of the United States, nor shall any state deprive any person of life, liberty or property without due process of law, nor deny to any person within its jurisdiction the equal protection of the laws."

It is not necessary to go into a discussion of the full scope of this amendment and the various decisions construing it. It is sufficient to say that it vests in the National Government the power and duty to protect, against the aggression of a State, every person within the jurisdiction of the United States in most of the personal rights, violation of which by Congress is forbidden in the first eight amendments to the Constitution.

The ninth amendment provided that the enumeration in the Constitution of certain rights should not be construed to deny or disparage others retained by the people, and the tenth laid down the rule of interpretation that the powers not delegated to the United States by the Constitution and not prohibited by it to the States were to be considered as reserved to the States respectively or to the people. These two clauses were intended to avoid too wide a construction of the national powers under the Constitution and were proposed and insisted upon by the followers of Jefferson.

The eleventh article provided that the judicial power of the United States should not be construed to extend to any suit in law or equity commenced or prosecuted against one of the United States by citizens of another State or by citizens or subjects of any foreign State. This was proposed at the first session of the third Congress, also by the followers of Jefferson, and was adopted to avoid the effect of the decision of the Supreme Court in Chisholm vs. Georgia in 1793, that a State might be sued by a citizen of another State. This amendment exalted the sovereignty of the States. One of usual attributes of sovereignty in a government is immunity from suit in its courts. The amendment was, therefore, a victory for the States' rights men and for the narrower view of the Constitution.

From the first, then, the issue was as to what kind of "a more perfect union" had been established. Jefferson had not been a member of the

struction of the Constitution, the effect of that
instrument would have been determined by the
independent and varying judgments of the several
States, and our union would have been treated as
a compact of sovereign members, rather than as a
sovereign nation. From time to time, Jefferson
and his successors appointed judges upon the
Supreme Court with a view to neutralizing the
influence and views of Marshall. But so strong
was the personality of the great Chief Justice, so
powerful his intellectual force, so clear his statesmanlike conviction that this was and must be a
nation, that enough of the new men put upon the
Court were changed to his view to keep the States'
rights men always in the minority, and the control
of Marshall continued until his death in the administration of Andrew Jackson.

In the case of Marbury vs. Madison, Marshall
laid down the proposition which insured the
power of the Federal Supreme Court to declare
invalid any law of Congress which was held by the
Court to be in violation of the Constitution. This
doctrine was denounced by Jefferson as a usurpation by the Court. In Cohens vs. Virginia, the
Chief Justice announced the supremacy of the
Federal Supreme Court in the consideration of
Federal questions and its power to overrule the
decisions of a Supreme Court of a State in such

matters and to set aside the law of a State which was in conflict with the Federal Constitution. In McCulloch vs. Maryland and in Osborn vs. the Bank, the same great jurist, as the organ of the Court, settled for all time the liberal construction of the Constitution in conferring powers upon the National Government to be implied from the express powers. The Court refused to limit the implication of powers to those which were indispensable to the exercise of the express powers, but held that any method of carrying out the express powers which was reasonably proper and adapted to the purpose, was in the discretion of Congress.

When Jefferson and Madison as political factors were seeking to minimize the national powers under the Constitution, they were merely representing the spirit of state sovereignty which was strong in Jefferson, because he feared danger to individual rights and a monarchical tendency in a national construction of the Constitution. In communications to Congress, in published letters, and in every other way, he thundered against the power of the Supreme Court and the construction that it was putting upon the Constitution in exalting and broadening the national sovereignty and minimizing the power of the States. But it was all to no purpose, and he had the irritating disappointment of finding his own appointees, as I have already indicated, concurring in the views of Marshall and making the decisions of the Supreme Court consistent from the first in a Federalistic construction of the fundamental instrument of government. The school of Jefferson was continued by Calhoun, the great rival of Webster, one of the greatest statesmen of any time, and one of the strongest logicians and political writers. Calhoun attempted in South Carolina to set at naught the collection of customs duties, on the ground that the Federal customs law violated the Constitution. In doing this, he encountered a vigorous assertion of national authority by Andrew Jackson. But, on the other hand, Andrew Jackson denounced the construction of the Supreme Court, which upheld the legislation establishing a United States Bank, and refused to recognize the law as valid, or to follow the Court's decision. But the judgments of the Supreme Court were permanent, and while one President nullified or disregarded them, others succeeded and ultimately the view of the Court was established.

When Marshall died in 1835, the question of anti- and pro-slavery had come to be the chief issue before the people of the United States. And the tendency of the dominant Democratic party was toward the maintenance of slavery as entitled to protection under the Constitution. The slave-holding party was strong in its wish to extend slave-holding territory with a view to spreading the doctrine and strengthening its influence. In Section 2, Article 4, the Constitution of the United States provides as follows:

"No person held to service or labor in one state under the laws thereof, escaping into another, shall in consequence of any law or regulation therein be discharged from such service or labor, but shall be delivered up on claim of the party to whom such service or labor may be due."

Under the authority of this provision Congress passed what was known as the fugitive slave law.

It ought to be said that Jefferson and Madison were by no means pro-slavery men. Jefferson was anxious that slavery should be abolished, and it could almost be said that early in the constitutional and political history of this country there was no tense issue in respect to slavery. The slave trade in the United States, the Constitution provided, might be forbidden by Congress after 1808. The States' rights attitude of neither Jefferson nor Madison could be attributed to the influence of this issue. However, the development of the cotton industry through the South through the invention of the cotton gin, and the supposed necessity for the use of slave labor in raising cotton, gave to the South a strong interest in maintaining it as a social institution, and made its preservation the chief feature in the Democratic party's doctrine.

When, therefore, the slave property became valuable, as it did in the time of Jackson and later, the enforcement of the fugitive slave law became most important to the pro-slavery party in Congress and in the nation. Chief Justice Taney, who succeeded Marshall, and the other members of the Supreme Court, therefore, found no difficulty, Democrats as a majority of them were, in maintaining the supremacy of national authority upon State territory in the execution of laws passed in pursuance of the constitutional power and duty of Congress to provide for the return of fugitive slaves.

Decisions made on this subject strengthened the national construction of the Constitution by the Supreme Court in spite of the division in the Democratic party, and in spite of the contention by the southern branch of the party that secession was constitutional, and properly within the power of the States choosing to resort to it. Indeed the fugitive slave law put the abolitionists and those who sympathized with them in the attitude, temporary though it was, of opposition to the national authority on State soil.

Thus by a series of fortuitous circumstances, the construction of the Constitution has always been entrusted to a court that was naturally inclined to uphold the national power and not to emphasize unduly the sovereignty of the States.

When the war came on, the question submitted to the arbitrament of war was the right of secession, and that of course was decided in the negative by the result at Appomattox. Since then no question has been made by any party or school of politics as to the views that Marshall enforced— in respect to the national power.

This history is a striking tribute to the power of the Supreme Court in shaping the destinies of the nation and to the law-abiding character of the people of the country in that, however much political parties may have temporarily differed from the judgments of that Court, those judgments have ultimately prevailed.

Of course there was the Dred Scott decision, involving the status of a free negro as to citizenship, which, delivered late in the fifties, aroused the indignation of the anti-slavery party against Chief Justice Taney and the majority of the Court, and called forth the careful but forcible criticism of Lincoln and the unmeasured abuse of the abolitionists. That question, however, was removed from judicial controversy by the war and the war amendments to the Constitution, and at any rate had only indirect bearing on the main question of the rights of the States and the powers of the general Government.

Circumstances in the growth of the country have served greatly to increase the volume of Federal power. This has not come from a new construction of the Constitution, but it has come from the fact that the Federal power has been enlarged by the expansion of the always conceded subjects of national activities. It is true that there was a judgment of the Supreme Court as far back as 1846, in the case of the Genesee Chief— Chief Justice Taney delivering the decision—which had the effect to increase largely the Federal jurisdiction in one direction. The maritime jurisdiction of the admiralty courts in England had been limited to tidal waters because in England no other waters were navigable. In the United States, however, there were thousands of miles of river navigation and lake navigation that were beyond the reach of ocean tides. The question was whether the maritime jurisdiction of the United States Government reached to navigable rivers and lakes. Congress passed a law extending the jurisdiction of the Federal Admiralty Courts to such waters and the Supreme Court sustained the law, reversing some decisions that tended to another view. This was one apparent enlargement of Federal jurisdiction in the history of the Supreme Court, but it was a natural and necessary application of the Constitution in the light of the common law and its proper adaptation to our circumstances. It is this power which now places all navigable rivers and harbors within the control of the United States, and leads to the passage of the rivers and harbors bills appropriating money for their improvement, with a view to their navigation.

A great increase in the volume of Federal jurisdiction not due to an enlargement of its defined limits, but due to the increase of business within those limits, arises from the power given to Congress by the Constitution to regulate commerce between the States, with the Indian tribes and with foreign nations. As I have stated, it was the interference with interstate commerce by State obstruction that was one of the chief reasons for bringing the people together into the formation of a Federal Constitution. Originally the business between the States was considerably less than the business done within the States, so that the national control of interstate commerce seemed less important than regulation by the States of their own commerce. But with the invention of steam navigation of waters, and with the construction of railroads, the interstate commerce of the country has increased from one-fourth of the entire country's commerce to three-fourths of it.

In 1887 a law was passed organizing the Interstate Commerce Commission, and delegating to it certain regulative powers in respect to railroad rates in traffic between the States. This law has been amended and reamended and amended again until now the control exercised over interstate commerce by the Interstate Commerce Commission, when that commerce is carried by railroads, is rounded and complete in the regulation of rates, and in other matters affecting the interest of the public. Regulation of express companies and of telegraph and telephone companies in their interstate business has also been entrusted to the Commission.

Then again, the necessities of modern government and the tendency toward greater paternalism have induced Congress to vest, by statute, in the general Government, powers that under the Constitution were impliedly within congressional creation, but which had been allowed to lie dormant in view of the supposed lack of public necessity for their exercise. Thus, as an outgrowth of the power of regulating commerce, comes the antitrust act, which forbids the organization of business combinations to do an interstate commerce business by combinations or conspiracies in restraint of interstate trade, or to establish monopolies therein. This has thrown into Federal jurisdiction a most important power, the exercise of which is now revolutionizing and purifying business methods and ridding them of unfair competition, of unjust suppression of fair competition, and of irresponsible but powerful monopolies and private despotisms in each large branch of industry. These colossal combinations are gradually being dissolved under the influence of the antitrust law and the action of our Federal Courts.

Another great addition to the volume of Federal jurisdiction has arisen under the same clause of the Constitution in the adoption of the pure food act. The Federal Government has no power to interfere with the food products grown or made and used in a State, but it has the power to regulate commerce between the States and to say what are proper subjects of that commerce, and to prevent the use of interstate commerce for the circulation of that which may injure the people reached through such commerce. It, therefore, has the power to insist that shippers shall comply with the regulations looking to the purity of the food products and of the drugs and medicines which they make the subjects of interstate commerce.

Bills have been urged upon Congress to forbid interstate commerce in goods made by child labor. Such proposed legislation has failed chiefly because it was thought beyond the Federal power. The distinction between the power exercised in enacting the pure food bill and that which would have been necessary in the case of the child labor bill is that Congress in the former is only preventing interstate commerce from being a vehicle for conveyance of something which would be injurious to people at its destination, and it might properly decline to permit the use of interstate commerce for that detrimental result. In the latter case, Congress would be using its regulative power of interstate commerce not to effect any result of interstate commerce. Articles made by child labor are presumably as good and useful as articles made by adults. The proposed law is to be enforced to discourage the making of articles by child labor in the State from which the articles were shipped. In other words, it seeks indirectly and by duress, to compel the States to pass a certain kind of legislation that is completely within their discretion to enact or not. Child labor in the State of the shipment has no legitimate or germane relation to the interstate commerce of which the goods thus made are to form a part, to its character or to its effect. Such an attempt of Congress to use its power of regulating such commerce to suppress the use of child labor in the State of shipment would be a clear usurpation of that State's rights.

Another recent increase in the volume of Federal business is due to an application of the same clause of the Constitution to what is known as the white slave business, that is, the transfer of women from one State to another for purposes of prostitution and the spread of vice.

Take another instance under another head of Federal jurisdiction. The post office has proved a most convenient means of perpetrating fraud by sending letters to people who, influenced by false pretenses contained in the letters, part with their money. This has led to a statute punishing those who use the post office to defraud. Acts of this sort are generally cognizable in the State as the crime of obtaining money under false pretenses. The fact, however, that the scheme is usually a conspiracy that covers many States, and that there is difficulty in securing the necessary witnesses in a State court has brought into the Federal Court a large volume of business of this kind.

Then within the last Administration, the functions of the Post Office Department have been extended to include the maintenance of Postal Savings Banks and a Parcels Post. These new enterprises are bound to involve wider Federal usefulness and greater manifestation of Federal authority.

The addition to the business of the National Government in its executive and judicial branches, due to the enforcement of all these statutes, is enormous and is an explanation of why the central Government seems to have grown at the expense of the States.

Moreover, the Spanish War thrust on the Government at Washington the full care and supervision of the Philippines and Porto Rico, and their population of 9,000,000 of people. The Platt Amendment gives a quasi-governmental responsibility in Cuba. Then the construction and maintenance of the Panama Canal and the government of the Canal Zone increase greatly the volume of our strictly national affairs.

This great expansion of Federal activities has been almost within the present generation and within the recollection, and by the agency, of living men; but it has not changed the form of our government, nor has it lessened our obligation to respect the sovereign rights of the State.

This brings me to a consideration of the importance of maintaining the constitutional autonomy of our States. Our Federal system is the only form of popular government that would be possible in a country like ours, with an enormous territory and 100,000,000 population. There is a great homogeneity among the people, greater indeed than many of us suppose, but, on the other hand, not only the mere geographical differences, but the differing interests of the people in different localities, require that a certain part of their government should be clearly within their own local control and not subject to the interference of people living at a great distance from them. But for this safety valve by which people of one State can have such State government as they choose, we would never be able to keep the union of all the people so harmonious as we now have. The friction that would occur between different parts of the country under any other system is well illustrated by the working out of the issue of national conservation.

The public domain in lands west of the Mississippi and Missouri rivers was changed into private ownership through the homestead law, the pre-emption acts, the grants to the Pacific Railroads, the stone and timber act, the reclamation act and other land legislation. The administration of these acts was not rigid, but lax in accord with the public sentiment of the people who were pioneering and forgot everything in the zeal for expanding the settlement of the country. About seven years ago the whole country woke up to the fact that vast areas had passed to private and corporate ownership without compliance with law and that much of the valuable land of the government had gone. The necessity for preserving the forests pressed itself upon the minds of all the people and there came a public demand for stricter enforcement of the land laws, for recovery of those lands lost through fraud that could be recovered and the punishment of the conspirators in the fraud. The cry was for national conservation and a very necessary and useful doctrine it has proved to be.

Now that the sharpness of the public attention in the East has been somewhat abated, there has come from the West a complaint that finds support in all the public land States that a certain rigidity and delay in making patents under the land laws have created a halt in development wherever the public domain is found, and that the withdrawal of coal lands, oil and gas lands, phosphate lands, water power sites, with a view to the passage of a conservation law for leasing rather than selling outright these sources of national wealth, growing more valuable every day, is a wrong policy and

that the people of the States where these lands
are should now be given an opportunity quickly
to acquire the necessary title to them and to
develop them and expand the productiveness of
those States. The feeling is becoming more acute
and the politics of whole States are turning upon
it. Some reasonable adjustment of the trouble
will have to be reached. The case is an exception
because generally matters having such an immediate local importance are within the control of
the people of the State. But the asperity and
vigor of the complaints illustrate very well the
inevitable result if everything were regulated
from Washington and the State governments
were reduced to nothing but agencies of the
National Government.

Again, the great financial resources available to
the Federal Government by use of its taxing power
offer a temptation to those who would spend for
local purposes without the burden of paying heavy
taxes at home. The South with its natural political tendencies and as the result of its political
history would be naturally in favor of a strict
view as to what are proper objects of national
expenditure, but since the abolition of slavery and
since the disappearance of the political issue as
to the voting of the negroes in the South, in other
words, since the practical nullification of the fif-

teenth amendment in those States, there has been
a revolution of feeling and a strong impulse on
the part of southern politicians to favor national
legislation to accomplish many purposes which
had been denounced as unconstitutional in earlier
days.   In other words, we find from the South and
from the West a willingness to have the National
Government spend a large part of its receipts in
enterprises that will inure to the benefit of the
State communities and will be paid for more
largely by people living in States not benefited
than by the people of the States which are.

This has been one of the criticisms directed
against the river and harbor bills and against
public buildings bills.   They have been called the
"pork barrel" bills.   They have been usually
attacked in those parts of the country that had
to furnish most of the "pork" and got little of it,
that is, the populous Eastern and Middle States.
There are now organizations in the older part of
the country whose purpose is to devise plans for
Federal improvements there which will give the
people of that section what is regarded as their
share.

Criticism of public improvement bills is not,
however, always just.   There are enterprises so
national in their character and effect that people
remote from them geographically are still very

beneficially affected. Such I conceive to be a comprehensive plan for keeping the Mississippi within its banks, to be contributed to by the States but to be executed under Federal authority.

In the reclamation law for the irrigation of arid public lands in Western States, the money expended was to be expended from a fund to be made up of the proceeds of sales of public lands in those States, and from the water rents and assessments upon the irrigated lands. Thus the burden on the general Government was localized and confined to government lands in the States benefited. These proceeds have been anticipated by issuing $20,000,000 bonds, but as they are to be paid out of funds raised as above described, the fairness of the reclamation plan can hardly be questioned.

Other expenditures now proposed can not be so justified, however. There is now being agitated and advocated a plan to build good roads in all the States of the United States, the fund for the purpose to be contributed to by the general Government and the States. Under the plan, the State of New York would receive from the fund just about one-half the sum to be awarded to Nevada, while New York's contribution would be many times that of Nevada. This is unjust and is dangerous. While there is probably no doubt of

the power of the National Government to build
wagon roads from one State to another, roads of
this character are so much a matter of local concern, and the interstate traffic is so largely taken
care of by railroads and river and sea navigation,
that I believe it to be most unwise for the general
Government to indulge in road building.   The
States should do it.   The older States have already taken up the work and the rest should
follow them.   The evils of "pork barrel" bills in
rivers and harbors appropriations, and in public
buildings bills will seem small and inconsiderable
in the mad chase for a share in the good roads
bills which the imaginations of many Congressmen
have already made into law.

The same proposal is being made in respect to
the draining of the swamp lands of the various
States.   Most of these lands were given by the
central Government to the States and much profit
has been made out of them.   If what remain unsold
are to be drained, let the States do it, who own
them; or let them reconvey them to the United
States Government which may then drain them
as a profitable investment in improving its own
property if it is found to be such.

It is to be remembered that in the expenditure
of the people's money in the United States Treasury, Congress is a law unto itself in that it exer-

cises complete discretion to say what is a proper national purpose. Such a question can never come before the Supreme Court. This is very different from the exercise of Congress of the power of taxation. That affects individual right directly. Any complaining tax-payer may, therefore, at once invoke the judgment of the courts on the validity of a tax law. The distinction gives additional importance to public scrutiny of the purposes to which the Nation's funds are applied.

In the pursuit of home popularity by Congressional representatives by securing national appropriations for local purposes, and in the effort to avoid legitimate State expenditure by loading undue burdens on the general Government, there is danger that the States will lose their dignity and power. Such dangerous proposals, however, find much support in the present temper of pseudo-reformers and demagogues who would rejoice in any governmental effort, however unfair, to take from those who have, and give to those who have not.

It is essential, therefore, in the life of our dual government that the power and functions of the State governments be maintained in all the fulness that they were intended to have by the framers of the Constitution. This is true not only for reasons I have given, but because the tendency to enlarge the constitutional authority and duties of the National Government has gone far beyond the mere expenditure of money.

A school has arisen called the New Nationalist School that proposes to put into operation a great many new remedies through the National Government, basing the national authority on the failure or unfitness of the States to discharge their proper and exclusive duties under the Constitution. This school is one which is closely associated with that which is trying to enforce new doctrines as to the direct rule of the people and an unsettling of the security of individual rights. Its members are generally impatient with the suggestion that certain reforms can only be effected through the State governments. They are in favor of national "hair trigger" legislation, and anything that has to depend upon the action of the forty-eight different States can never be of that kind.

To one opposed to the adoption of such remedies as I have been commenting on, the existence of the State governments is one of the chief grounds for hope that the tendency to error in the weakening of constitutional guaranties that is now going on in some States may be halted by the conservatism of other States, and that the errors from actual experience in departing from representative government in the more radical States will ultimately bring back the whole nation to sounder views.

I favor the principle of a graduated income tax. I urged the sixteenth amendment upon Congress in order to add to the nation's tax resources. But the present law was avowedly passed only to reduce the fortunes of the rich. It will not do so materially. There is a power in the State governments of reducing or dividing these fortunes in a practical way. Each State has complete control over the testamentary privilege given to any owner of property and may take away the power of leaving it all to one child or require that it be left in some other way, and this without the violation of any of the guaranties of the Constitution. Now, if this be true, why has it not been proposed in some State? First, because the "hair trigger" reformer desires to reform the entire country at onc and wishes to seem to do it in a way to attract attention and support a national party. Second, because no State, however bitter against its own rich men, would wish to deprive itself of their residence and of their tax-producing quality by passing a law which would drive them into some other State where the devolution of property is more in accordance with previous tradition and custom. Therefore, while this power to reduce the possibility of the accumulation of great fortunes and their maintenance through two or three generations is completely within the action of the States, not a single State has attempted it.

The experience of Kansas and some of the other States, where populism ran riot for a time, is instructive. Then everyone was against the creditor and in favor of the debtor and wished to put obstacles in the path of the former in seeking to recover his money when due. To gratify the popular demand, the legislature passed stay laws which introduce many delays in the legal procedure of the State for the collection of mortgages. The people of Kansas learned a lesson from the result of such legislation that has not yet been forgotten. Capital fled the State of Kansas as men flee from a contagious disease and business became as dead in Kansas as if it had no population at all. The blight that followed taught the statesmen of that State the utilitarian doctrine that honesty is the best policy, and that laws that drove creditors from a State and frightened away all capital, helped neither those who owed money nor those who did not owe money in the State. These so-called remedial laws were very soon repealed and since then other States have not made exactly the same mistake, though there are similar lessons in store for many of them.

There is a great advantage in having different State governments try different experiments in the enactment of laws and in governmental policies, so that a State less prone to accept novel and untried remedies may await their development by States more enterprising and more courageous. The end is that the diversity of opinion in State governments enforces a wise deliberation and creates a *locus pœnitentiœ* which may constitute the salvation of the Republic.

VII

"To Establish Justice"

The next reason for ordaining the Constitution as stated in the preamble was "to establish justice." There were courts in each State exercising general jurisdiction under its authority. The establishment of justice referred to in the preamble was the creation of courts under the authority of the new National Government to hear causes that involved its laws, and also to supplement the work of the courts of the various States by providing tribunals for ordinary litigation which should be indifferent as between citizens of different States. The Constitution could not properly remit to State tribunals the exercise of all judicial power. Such an arrangement would make the new government lack dignity and the usual functions of a sovereign, and more than that, there would be no final and supreme tribunal to settle questions of Federal law where the Supreme Courts of the State might differ.

The Constitution provides that there shall be one Supreme Court, and such inferior courts as Congress may from time to time ordain and establish. It also defines what the judicial power of the United States is or may extend to, thus giving the limitations of the jurisdiction that Congress may confer upon courts it creates. Under the Constitution, except in suits between States and in suits by Ambassadors, the Supreme Court can not hear suits as brought, but has jurisdiction only to review the decisions of other courts.

While the Constitution provided for one Supreme Court, it did not limit the number of Judges. It was, therefore, for Congress to provide what number of Supreme Court Judges there might be. This very important power Congress has, at times, threatened with partisan zeal to abuse. It has been once or twice proposed to change the supposed political complexion of the Court by creating additional judgeships. Every patriot sincerely hopes that Congress may never be moved to adopt such a course. The number of Judges originally was seven. It was then reduced to five. The number has been changed from time to time, and now the number is nine.

The original judiciary act was drafted by Oliver Ellsworth. He was a member of the Constitutional Convention and of the United States Senate from Connecticut. Upon the committee with him were three or four other members of the Constitutional Convention, from which it is to be inferred that the act properly carried out the purposes of that framing body. Mr. Ellsworth subsequently became Chief Justice of the United States, but his greatest public service for which he is chiefly remembered was his judiciary act. While the judiciary act has been amended from time to time, it still retains much of its original language and form. It established, as inferior courts, in each of the circuits, now numbering nine, a district court and a circuit court and defined their jurisdictions, and provided for the appellate jurisdiction of the Supreme Court. In 1892, an intermediate appellate court, called the Circuit Court of Appeals, was created in each circuit. In 1911, the jurisdiction of the circuit courts was transferred to the district courts and the circuit courts were abolished.

The Constitution makes the tenure of office of a judge during good behavior, which means during his life, provided he be not impeached. It provides that his compensation shall never be diminished during his term of office, and in this way he is made as independent as possible of the legislative or executive power after he has once been appointed and confirmed by the Senate. I shall comment on the beneficial effect of these provisions in a later chapter.

Congress has passed a law providing that all

Federal Judges may retire after a service of ten years upon attaining the age of seventy. The law is in form not compulsory because I presume it was thought doubtful whether Congress had any power to retire Judges, even though they continue the full salary as a life pension. I think the absence of power in Congress to do this is a defect. There is no doubt that there are Judges at seventy who have ripe judgments, active minds, and much physical vigor, and that they are able to perform their judicial duties in a very satisfactory way. Yet in a majority of cases when men come to be seventy, they have lost vigor, their minds are not as active, their senses not as acute, and their willingness to undertake great labor is not so great as in younger men, and as we ought to have in Judges who are to perform the enormous task which falls to the lot of Supreme Court Justices. In the public interest, therefore, it is better that we lose the services of the exceptions who are good Judges after they are seventy and avoid the presence on the Bench of men who are not able to keep up with the work, or to perform it satisfactorily. The duty of a Supreme Judge is more than merely taking in the point at issue between the parties, and deciding it. It frequently involves a heavy task in reading records and writing opinions. It thus is a substantial drain upon one's energy.

When most men reach seventy, they are loath thoroughly to investigate cases where such work involves real physical endurance.

I don't know that there is any method, except by a change of the Constitution, for remedying the defect that I have suggested. It has sometimes been proposed that, as the retirement pension is optional with Congress, it be granted on condition that the Judge retires at seventy, and if he does not then retire, but delays his retirement until after he has become somewhat older, he shall not have the privilege of retirement on a pension. This it is thought would frighten Judges into an acceptance of the Congressional pension at the right age. I doubt if anything could be accomplished by such legislation.

I would certainly not agitate now the question of amending the Constitution in respect to the tenure of the Federal Judges, because it would be dangerous in the present hysterical condition of many people, and a movement would at once be set on foot not only to retire Judges at seventy, but to make them elective and to give them short terms. Hence, for the present, we can afford to continue to leave the matter to the good sense of the Judges themselves. I ought to add, however, that the experience of men, close to the Court, in respect to the willingness of the Judges to retire after they have become seventy, has not been very different from that of Gil Blas with the Bishop.

I shall not read at length the article defining the judicial power. It is sufficient to say for our purposes that it extends to all cases involving the construction of the Constitution of the United States and the statutes and treaties of the United States, in other words, to the enforcement of Federal law as distinguished from State law; and, secondly, that it includes the consideration of all kinds of litigation between citizens of different States.

It is difficult for us who have been born and brought up in an atmosphere of the Federal and State courts to realize how complicated and almost unintelligible our judicial system is to foreigners. They find it difficult to understand dual governmental authority in which, over the same territory, courts may exercise the same kind of jurisdiction concurrently, and yet act under different sovereignties. I have already stated the reasons for the establishment of a Federal judicial system. I need not further refer to the necessity for a national tribunal to settle finally national questions. The other reason requires a little further comment. Those who framed and adopted the Constitution feared that the citizen of one State seeking to assert his rights in another State be-

fore the courts of that other State, might find
himself prejudicially affected by the local feeling
in favor of a resident and against a non-resident,—in favor of a citizen against a non-citizen.
It was, therefore, given to Congress to establish
inferior courts in every State so that in each
State a citizen of another State might have his
cause heard before a tribunal whose Judge, bearing the commission of the President of the nation
and exercising the authority of the National Government, would be presumed to be free from any
local feeling and to administer justice with entire
impartiality between litigants, whatever their residence or citizenship.   The effectiveness of this
provision and its wisdom have been fully vindicated by 125 years of actual experience.

The greatest function of the Federal Courts,
and especially of the Supreme Court, is the power
to declare void the laws either of Congress or of
the legislatures of the States which are found to
conflict with the provisions of the Constitution.

In England there had been some intimation by
Lord Chief Justice Holt and by Lord Chief Justice Coke that Courts had the right to disregard
acts of Parliament.   Coke said that the common
law controlled acts of Parliament and adjudged
them void when against common right and reason,
and Holt adopted this dictum of Coke which he

found to be supported by Lord Chief Justice Hobart, who, in a reported case, insisted that an act of Parliament made against natural equity so as to make a man judge in his own cause was void. But England is without a written constitution, and the generally accepted rule in English law is that Parliament is omnipotent and that the acts of Parliament must be enforced by the Courts and are beyond any criticism on their part or any power of theirs to declare the acts void.

In the United States, however, we have a written Constitution. It declares the fundamental law and it imposes limitations upon the powers of all branches of the Government. Now if any branch of the Government exceeds those powers to which it is thus limited, the act is without authority and must be void. The question is who is to determine whether the act does exceed the authority given. The action of the Supreme Court is confined to the hearing and decision of real litigated cases and the exercise of judicial power between parties. It is essential to the carrying out of this jurisdiction that the court should determine what the law is governing the issue between the litigants. Therefore, when a statute is relied upon by one party, and it is claimed by the other that the statute can have no effect because in violation of the fundamental law, the

Court must decide whether the statute was within the power of the legislature which passed it or not. That process of reasoning is the one pursued by Chief Justice Marshall in the case of Marbury vs. Madison. The reasoning has been accepted as sound in practice for 125 years and courts have exercised this authority, both the Supreme Court of the United States and the Supreme Court of States, for all that time.

The other theory is that it is for the branch of the Government exercising authority to determine whether it is acting within its authority or not, that its judgment on the subject is conclusive, and that any other branch of the Government having to investigate the validity of its act must accept the fact of its action as proof of its validity.

Experience has shown that the obligation to keep within the Constitution sits very lightly upon State legislatures and it is not always regarded by Congress. The people are temporarily moved to demand something which the Constitution forbids. It is argued with some force that if there were no method of resorting to the Courts to declare the invalidity of laws, the members of Congress or of the legislatures would be as careful to follow closely the limitations of their power as the British Parliament has been to follow the unwritten constitution of that country. The assumption that the Courts are the real arbiters as to the issue of the validity of a legislative act, it is said, lifts the responsibility from legislators and they, therefore, vote for the measures they favor without regard to constitutional restriction. I concede the force of this argument to the extent of admitting that both legislatures and Congress are not as sensitive to their constitutional obligations as they ought to be, and they are quite willing to shift the burden of defeating popular measures to the judicial tribunals. But we can not safely assume that if the decision of the legislatures or Congress were final as to validity of laws, and there could be no resort to the Courts, temporary but powerful pressure in favor of infringements of the Constitution contained in legislation pleasing to the constituencies would not prevail.

To contend that the Courts have no power whatever to consider the validity of laws passed by a legislature or Congress under a written Constitution is much too extreme a doctrine. We may admit that some courts have gone too far in the exercise of this power. They ought not to exercise it, except when the conflict between the Constitution and the act whose validity is in question are irreconcilable. The violation of the constitutional limitation must be plainly beyond the

permissible discretion of the legislature in interpreting its own powers under the Constitution.
Courts ought not to set aside a law when there is
room for difference of opinion as to its validity,
and though the Court, in passing on the matter
as an original question, might think it crosses the
line, it must accept the view of the legislature as
most persuasive of the view that what it has done
is within the permissive limits of its discretion. In
other words, the invalidity of a law solemnly
adopted by the legislature given authority to
enact laws should not be declared, unless the want
of power appears to be beyond reasonable doubt.

The modern argument against the action of the
Courts in holding laws to be invalid is that it gives
to them a political and legislative power and
deprives the people of that which should be theirs.
One enthusiast in the crusade against the Courts
has pointed out that 458 acts of legislatures had
been declared invalid by the State and Federal
Courts during a recent year, and has concluded
that the Courts are thus exercising enormous political and legislative power. He insists that such
power ought to rest with the people and, therefore, that such decisions of the courts should be
referred to the electorate at the next election.

An argument like this does not appeal to any
one who understands the facts. The general run

of cases presenting the issue of validity or non-validity, under a fundamental law, does not involve politics at all or anything like legislative discretion. It involves only a lawyer-like construction of the Constitution and the law in question to decide whether they are in conflict. I doubt not that of the 458 cases, nearly all were cases of palpable violation of the fundamental law which it was a purely non-political, judicial function for the Courts to recognize and declare. In the remainder, there may have been questions which were economical or political in the larger sense. I mean by this, political in the general view of the powers of the National Government and not political in the sense of partisan politics of a temporary color. They may have involved the extent of the police power of government and its proper curtailment of individual rights.

If, in the latter very small class of cases, the people differ from the construction put by the Courts upon such a question, they still have the authority to amend the Constitution and make it so plain that no court can ignore it.

Checks upon the action of the people in amending their constitutions have been imposed with a view to secure full information and deliberation on the part of the people, and certainly both those things are essential to a safe amendment of the fundamental law. It only means delay in a radical change and when we consider how short a period a decade is in the life of a nation, a delay of two or three years is not only tolerable but ought to be necessary. I shall consider the general attack on so-called judge-made law later on in this volume.

I now come to consider two new remedies for supposed evils growing out of our judicial system, State and national. I refer to the popular recall of judicial officers and the popular recall of judicial decisions. I shall discuss these in their order.

The popular recall of judges has been put into effect in several States and it was made part of the constitution of Arizona tendered for approval, when her people in convention asked for admission to statehood. I vetoed the bill admitting her on the ground that the proposed constitution contained this provision. Congress then made the admission conditional on the people's striking out this clause of the constitution and the people did so. Promptly upon admission, however, the clause was restored to their constitution by the people of the State. I do not think I can better state my views on this subject than by an extended quotation from my message to Congress vetoing the Arizona bill, in which I said:

"The Constitution distributes the functions of government into three branches—the legislative, to make the laws; the executive, to execute them; and the judicial, to decide in cases arising before it the rights of the individual as between him and others and as between him and the government. This division of government into three separate branches has always been regarded as a great security for the maintenance of free institutions, and the security is only firm and assured when the judicial branch is independent and impartial. The executive and legislative branches are representative of the majority of the people which elected them in guiding the course of the government within the limits of the Constitution. They must act for the whole people, of course; but they may properly follow, and usually ought to follow, the views of the majority which elected them in respect to the governmental policy best adapted to secure the welfare of the whole people.

"But the judicial branch of the government is not representative of a majority of the people in any such sense, even if the mode of selecting judges is by popular election. In a proper sense, judges are servants of the people; that is, they are doing work which must be done for the government, and in the interest of all the people, but it is not work in the doing of which they are to

follow the will of the majority, except as that is
embodied in statutes lawfully enacted according to
constitutional limitations.   They are not popular
representatives.   On the contrary, to fill their
office properly, they must be independent.   They
must decide every question which comes before
them according to law and justice.   If this question is between individuals, they will follow the
statute, or the unwritten law, if no statute applies,
and they take the unwritten law growing out of
tradition and custom from previous judicial decisions.   If a statute or ordinance affecting a cause
before them is not lawfully enacted, because it
violates the Constitution adopted by the people,
then they must ignore the seeming statute and
decide the question as if the statute had never been
passed.

"What I have said has been to little purpose if
it has not shown that judges to fulfill their functions properly in our popular government must
be more independent than in any other form of
government, and that need of independence is
greatest where the individual is one litigant, and
the State, guided by the successful and governing
majority, is the other.   In order to maintain the
rights of the minority and the individual and to
preserve our constitutional balance we must have

judges with courage to decide against the majority when justice and law require.

"By the recall in the Arizona Constitution, it is proposed to give to the majority power to remove arbitrarily and without delay any judge who may have the courage to render an unpopular decision. By the recall it is proposed to enable a minority of 25 per cent of the voters of the district or State, for no prescribed cause, after the judge has been in office six months, to submit the question of his retention in office to the electorate. The petitioning minority must say in their petition what they can against him in 200 words, and he must defend as best he can in the same space. Other candidates are permitted to present themselves and have their names printed on the ballot, so that the recall is not based solely on the record or the acts of the judge, but also on the question whether some other and more popular candidate has been found to unseat him. Could there be a system more ingeniously devised to subject judges to momentary gusts of popular passion than this?

"We can not be blind to the fact that often an intelligent and respectable electorate may be so roused upon an issue that it will visit with condemnation the decision of a just judge, though exactly in accord with the law governing the case, merely because it affects unfavorably their contest. Controversies over elections, labor troubles, racial or religious issues, issues as to the construction or constitutionality of liquor laws, criminal trials of popular or unpopular defendants, the removal of county seats, suits by individuals to maintain their constitutional rights in obstruction of some popular improvement—these and many other cases could be cited in which a majority of a district electorate would be tempted by hasty anger to recall a conscientious judge if the opportunity were open all the time.

"No period of delay is interposed for the abatement of popular feeling. The recall is devised to encourage quick action, and to lead the people to strike while the iron is hot. The judge is treated as the instrument and servant of a majority of the people and subject to their momentary will. Not after a long term in which his qualities as judge and his character as a man have been subjected to a test of all the varieties of judicial work and duty so as to furnish a proper means of measuring his fitness for continuance in another term, but on the instant of an unpopular ruling, while the spirit of protest has not had time to cool and even while an appeal may be pending from his ruling in which he may be sustained, he is to be haled before the electorate as a tribunal, with no judicial hearing, evidence or defence, and thrown out of office and disgraced for life because he has failed, in a single decision, it may be, to satisfy the popular demand.

"Attempt is made to defend the principle of judicial recall by reference to States in which judges are said to have shown themselves to be under corrupt corporate influence, and in which it is claimed that nothing but a desperate remedy will suffice. If the political control in such States is sufficiently wrested from corrupting corporations to permit the enactment of a radical Constitutional amendment, like that of judicial recall, it would seem possible to make provision, in its stead, for an effective remedy by impeachment in which the cumbrous features of the present remedy might be avoided, but the opportunity for judicial hearing and defence before an impartial tribunal might be retained. Real reforms are not to be effected by patent short cuts, or by abolishing those requirements which the experience of ages has shown to be essential in dealing justly with every one. Such innovations are certain in the long run to plague the inventor or first user, and will come readily to the hand of the enemies and corrupters of society after the passing of the just popular indignation that prompted their adoption.

"Again judicial recall is advocated on the ground that it will bring the judges more into sympathy with the popular will and the progress of ideas among the people. It is said that now judges are out of touch with movements toward a wider democracy, and a greater control of governmental agencies in the interest and for the benefit of the people. The righteous and just course for a judge to pursue is ordinarily fixed by statute or clear principles of law, and the cases in which his judgment may be affected by his political, economic, or social views are infrequent. But even in such cases, judges are not removed from the people's influence. Surround the judiciary with all the safeguards possible, create judges by appointment, make their tenure for life, forbid diminution of salary during their term, and still it is impossible to prevent the influence of popular opinion from coloring judgments in the long run. Judges are men, intelligent, sympathetic men, patriotic men, and in these fields of the law in which the personal equation unavoidably plays a part, there will be found a response to sober popular opinion as it changes to meet the exigency of social, political and economic changes."

Recall of Judicial Decisions

The proposition for a recall of judicial decisions by a popular vote is so utterly at variance with any procedure that ever was suggested in respect to civilized government that it is hard to deal with it. It had its origin in the impatience felt by some reformers in the economic views of judges who held that a law imposing limitations upon the hours of work of people engaged in certain industries was an infringement upon their individual right of free labor. The reformers contend that the law should be sustained as a legitimate exercise of the police power of the Government. The suggestion that such a question should be ultimately left to a popular election is now sought to be bolstered up by a phrase in an opinion of Mr. Justice Holmes, in Noble State Bank vs. Haskell, 219 U. S., 104, in which he says: "It may be said in a general way that the police power extends to all the great public needs. . . . It may be put forth in aid of what is sanctioned by usage or held by the prevailing morality or strong and preponderant opinion to be greatly and immediately necessary to the public welfare." Again he says: "With regard to the police power, as elsewhere in the law, lines are pricked out by the gradual approach and contact of decisions on the opposing sides." I fancy that Mr. Justice Holmes was the most surprised man in the United States when he learned that this language of his had been used to justify the anomalous, I had almost said absurd, proposal that the decision of the Supreme Court of a State or of the United States, in a case between litigants involving the question of the validity of the exercise of the police power, should be submitted by referendum to the reviewing judgment of a single popular election.

This was the last thing which Mr. Justice Holmes or the Supreme Court, for whom he spoke, had in mind when he referred to a strong and preponderant public opinion. Such an election would indeed be a most ephemeral and unstable guide to determine how far a man's personal rights were to be modified in the interest of the public police power. If we can judge by actual experience under referendums of this general character, the election, if carried at all in favor of the police power, would be carried by a small minority of the electorate in the very probable failure of a majority of the electorate to go to the polls, and by a still smaller minority of the whole people whose settled view constitutes public opinion. It would be influenced by all kinds of irrelevant considerations and by campaign misrepresentations as to the facts and the real issue. Every circumstance, whether the unpopularity of a party litigant or the supposed pecuniary benefit to the people of the particular locality, or any other upon which an appeal to prejudice or selfish interest could be based, would be used to influence the election. It is difficult to state a fact less conclusive of "a strong and preponderant public opinion" than a single vote upon such an issue. What was in the mind of the learned Justice and of the Court for whom he spoke was a view entertained by most people, and evidenced by expressions of popular will in the press, in the pulpit, in juridical writings, as well as by legislative action and popular elections. All of these evidences should cover a period long enough to leave no doubt about the clarity of the opinion or its deliberate character. Such an opinion is not expressed in election controversy where the losing vote is substantial, but it is the result of a general and continued acquiescence that does not suggest a party division or a heated campaign.

The main argument used to sustain the recall of judicial decisions is that if the people are competent to establish a constitution, they are competent to interpret it and that this recall of decisions is nothing but the exercise of the power of interpretation. The fallacy of this argument should be manifest. The approval of general principles in a constitution, on the one hand, and the interpretation of a statute and consideration of its probable operation in a particular case and its possible infringement of a general principle, on the other, are very different things. The one is simple, the latter complex; and the latter, when submitted to a popular vote, is much more likely to be turned into an issue of general approval or disapproval of the act on its merits for the special purpose of its enactment and in its application to the particular case than upon its violation of the Constitution. Moreover, a popular majority does not generally ratify a constitution, or any principle of it, or amend its terms until after it has been adopted by a constitutional convention or a legislature, and the final approval is, and ought to be, surrounded with such checks and delays as to secure full information and deliberation. In other words, the course of procedure in the adoption of a constitution or amendment is radically different from that proposed in the hasty vote of a majority in recalling a particular judgment of a Court and is hedged about to avoid the very dangers that I have pointed out as likely to ensue were this inconceivable and outlandish plan incorporated in our judicial system.

The proper and reasonable method of avoiding the effect of a decision of the Supreme Court construing the Constitution, which the considerate judgment of the people holds to be contrary to the public good, is to treat the Constitution as construed in existing force, and to amend the

Constitution according to the provisions of the Constitution itself. That involves an ultimate submission to the people after full discussion and deliberation. Why is it necessary, therefore, to suggest such a clumsy, unsatisfactory and impracticable method?

How could uniformity of fundamental or any other kind of law be possible under such a system? No one would claim that uniformity would be the result from successive elections held in different years. Instead of a constitution, consistent in its construction and uniform in its application, it would be a government by special instances, a government that in the end necessarily leads to despotism.

When this remarkable device of recalling judicial decisions was first advanced, it was carefully limited in its application to the decisions of State Courts and to issues concerning the extent of the police power, but so well received have been the demagogic attacks upon our Courts made upon the political platform that now this novel invention has been extended to include the judgments of the Supreme Court of the United States and to embrace all of those which hold laws to be invalid because in violation of the Constitution.

Many of these judgments concern and enforce the guaranties of personal rights contained in the

Constitution and nullify statutes which infringe them. It follows that many of the decisions to be submitted under this plan to the learned and discriminating judicial judgment of a majority of the voters who take the trouble to vote, would present the issue as between the people in whose avowed interest the law in question was passed and the individual whose property rights are said to be unjustly affected by the law. On such an issue, with the opportunities for demagogic appeals to popular prejudice against the defendant who might be a corporation or a rich man, and in the confusion of an excited campaign, is there not great danger that individual property right would be ignored and the law in question which infringed it would be sustained? To what would this all necessarily lead? To confiscation and then to socialism. Indeed it is difficult to tell whether the recall of judicial decisions is not as socialistic as it is anarchistic.

In the first chapter I commented on the fact that popular government was only a means to an end, to wit, that of the happiness of all classes and individuals, that this end could best be reached by the rule of a majority of a large representative electorate restrained by a constitution, defining the authority of the branches of the Government and restricting the invasion by the electorate of certain declared individual rights necessary to preserve and protect individual effort, with a view to the progress and happiness of society and its members. We have seen that to enforce and secure these constitutional rights an independent judiciary was established as an instrument through which, on his own initiative, each individual could invoke adequate protection to his rights. This method of uniting popular control with self-imposed restraint through a constitution and an independent judiciary to enforce it, is the secret of the strength of our nation, and it explains why we have lived and grown stronger under the same Constitution in the face of all kinds of obstacles, including the greatest civil war in history, and the difficulties of a material expansion and growth of population beyond the dreams of the most imaginative statesman. This is what called forth the encomium of Lord Acton, the great historian, in the memorable sentences I quoted from him.

Now what do we have in the initiative, referendum and the two recalls urged by a school of men who profess to be friends of popular government and most concerned to promote the people's happiness? We have a system by which it is proposed not only to weaken and render nugatory the declared guaranties of personal rights and the constitutional restraints upon the electorate and its majority, but also to take away the power and independence of that branch of the Government, the judiciary, without which such guaranties and restraints would be written in water. It is not alone the popular control of laws and executive action that gives a Democracy strength and long life. It is its capacity to do justice to the individual and the minority. Lack of this is what destroyed ancient democracies. What preserves ours are those self-imposed popular restraints and practical means for enforcing them that keep the course of the majority of the controlling electorate just to all and each of the people.

There are real grounds for criticising our judicial system as a whole which the politicians and demagogues do not find so profitable to dwell upon, or to suggest remedies for. I concede that our judicial system is not perfect or as good as it can be, and ought to be made. I have been preaching reform in our judicial procedure for years, especially in the enforcement of the criminal law. In addresses and in presidential messages I have pointed out the great need for cheapening the cost of civil litigation and for expediting it so as to put as little a burden on the poor litigant as possible.

The ultra reformers, the "hair trigger" gentlemen, pay little attention to the tedious detail of reforming procedure so as to reduce the cost of litigation and to speed final judgments. This is really one of the greatest reforms now needed; and it will do the poor man more good ten times than the shining nostrums held out to him as a ground for electing their inventors. But the work of amending procedure and cutting down cost bills and of cutting out useless forms and delays in the law is not spectacular. It does not attract votes. Still the much-abused lawyers have through their Bar Associations made many useful recommendations of changes in procedure and are knocking at the door of Congress and legislatures to secure their adoption.

I do not think we need to be discouraged by the charges and threats made against our Courts, especially if we remedy their real defects by the reforms already pointed out. There have been many attacks upon Courts in the past. Jefferson and Jackson were both most severe in their criticisms of the Federal Judiciary, and both were as popular and influential with the people as any Presidents we have had. And yet the Courts survived their attacks and lived to maintain principles which they both held to be abhorrent, and subversive of the liberties of the people. The Dred Scott decision, the legal tender cases, the income tax decision and the Insular cases, in all

of which the judgment was carried by a bare
majority, subjected the Court to the bitter attack
of those who sympathized with the minority decisions, and in each period of agitation and conflict
people shook their heads and said that the authority of the Supreme Court had been much shaken.
Yet the tribunal has gone on its way discharging
its high function in the Government with patriotic
purpose to maintain its authority, and to preserve
the constitutional rights of the individual and the
form of government as prescribed by our fathers.
The Court lives to-day, strong, virile, patriotic
and able and willing to recognize progress, to
treat the Constitution as elastic enough to permit
a construction which will conform to the growth
and necessities of the country, to view constitutional restrictions with reasonable regard to the
changes which have taken place in our business
and in our society, and yet determined to enforce
the principles of individual right and the essential
limitations upon the branches of the Government
which are provided for in our fundamental law.
The greatest advantage of our plan of government over every other is the character of the
judicial power vested in the Supreme Court. The
statesmen and historians of Europe look upon it
with wonder and amazement, speak of it with
profound approval, and regard it as the chief

instrument in the maintenance of that self-restraint which the people of the United States have placed upon themselves and which has made this Government the admiration of intelligent critics the world over.

VIII

"To Establish Justice"—(Continued)
The Selection and Tenure of Judges

The most conspicuous feature of the new government under the Federal Constitution was its division into three parts—the legislative, the executive and the judicial. Experience has vindicated that division, except, it may be, that some lack of efficiency has shown itself in the absence of more useful co-operation between the executive and the legislative branches. The wisdom of keeping the executive and the legislative branches apart from the judiciary has, however, been confirmed by the event, not only under the American Constitution, but in England and in all the states under her flag. In the United States, where judicial systems have different degrees of this quality, permitting comparison, the greater the independence of the Courts the stronger their influence, and the more satisfactory their jurisdiction and administration of justice.

In a popular government, the most difficult problem is to determine a satisfactory method of selecting the members of its judicial branch. Where ought such power to be placed? It is a great one. It is said it ought not to be entrusted to irresponsible men. If this means that judges should not be men who do not understand the importance of the function they are exercising, or the gravity of the results their decision may involve, or do not exert energy and sincere intellectual effort to decide according to law and justice, every one must concur. But if it means that judges must be responsible for their judgments to some higher authority, so that for errors made in good faith they incur a personal liability, then we know from centuries of actual experience that the interest of justice, pure and undefiled, requires their immunity. Finality of decision is essential in every branch of the Government, or else government cannot go on. This is as true of its judiciary branch as of other branches. Therefore, somebody must have the final word in judicial matters, and the only question is who can best exercise this power. The answer to the question must be found in the real character of the function which the judges are to perform.

There is a school of political philosophers to-day who say that there are no positive standards of right and justice, but that these vary with the popular will, and that we are to learn what they are from its expression.

If right and justice are dependent on the votes of the electorate, and if what are known as individual rights are merely privileges held at the will of a majority, then the proposition that the judicial officer represents the people in the same sense as the executive officer, so that when the electoral majority differs from his judgment he ought to be removed, has some logical foundation. So, too, in this view, the proposition that the final decision of the courts shall be submitted on review to a popular election has reason in it.

But I shall assume, for the purposes of this discussion, that principles of right and justice and honesty and morality are not merely conventional and have a higher source than a plebiscite.

There is a broad field for the proper exercise of legislative power in prescribing rules of human conduct, and it is the function of courts to interpret them. This is the work of trained lawyers who know the theory and purpose of government, who are familiar with previous statutes, and who understand legislative methods of expression so that they can put themselves in the attitude of the legislature when it acted. When it is the duty of a court to say whether what was enacted by the legislature under the forms of law is within its power, it must discharge a delicate duty and one requiring in its members ability, learning and experience properly to interpret both the seeming law and the Constitution, and properly to measure what was within the permissible discretion of the legislature in construing its own authority. The majority of questions before our Courts, however, are neither statutory nor constitutional, but are dependent for decision upon the common or customary law handed down from one generation to another, adjusted to new conditions of society, and declared from time to time by courts as cases arise. Thorough study is required to enable a judge to know and understand the whole range of legal principles that have thus to be discriminatingly adapted and applied. Work of this kind requires professional experts of the highest proficiency, who have mastered the law as a science and in practice.

Where are we to get such experts? When a man of high character, ability and intelligence is to be selected for the chief executive office, the electorate can be safely charged with electing one from the necessarily few candidates who are sufficiently prominent. But what of the searching out in a large profession the best expert, the man with real learning, with judicial temperament, with

keenness of perception, with power of analysis
and nice distinction, with large technical experience? Can he be found better by election or by
appointment? There can be but one answer to
this query. The selection can be really popular
without resorting to an election. The Chief Executive elected by the people to represent them in
executive work does, in appointing a judge, execute the popular will. He can search among the
members of the Bar and can inform himself
thoroughly as to the one best qualified. Generally
he has sources of information, both of an open
and a confidential character, and if he is not
himself a lawyer or personally familiar with
the qualifications of the candidates, he has an
Attorney-General and other competent advisers
to aid him in the task.

For these reasons, in every country of the
world, except in the Cantons of Switzerland and
the United States, judges are appointed and not
elected. With us, in the decade between 1845 and
1855, when new constitutions were being adopted
in many States, a change was made to the elective
system. It was not an improvement. In some
States the change was not made. A comparison
between the work of the appointed judges and
of the elected judges shows that appointment
secures in the long run a higher average of

experts for the Bench. The principle of the short ballot, which is much put forward nowadays by reformers, and which thus far is much more honored by them in the breach than in the observance, really limits the election by the people to the Chief Executive and to legislators, and delegates to the elected Executive the appointment of all other officers, including the judiciary. The Executive who makes the appointments is properly held responsible to the public for the character of his selections.

We have had many able judges by popular election. These have owed their preferment to several circumstances. The effect of the old method of appointment was visible in the working of the new system for a decade or more, and good judges were continued by general acquiescence. In some States, indeed, the practice of re-electing judges without contest obtained until within recent years. Moreover, able judges have been nominated often through the influence of leading members of the Bar upon the politicians who controlled the nominations. Shrewd political leaders have not infrequently treated a judgeship as a non-political place, because the office has had comparatively little patronage. If the nominee has been a man of high quality, conspicuously fit, commanding the support of the professional and intelligent non-partisan votes, it has tended to help the rest of the ticket to success. The instances of great and able judges who have been placed on the Bench by election are instances of the adaptability of the American people and their genius for making the best out of bad methods, and are not a vindication of the system. That has resulted in the promotion to the judicial office of other judges who have impaired the authority of the courts by their lack of strength, clearness and courage, and who have shown neither a thorough knowledge of the customary law, nor a constructive faculty in the application of it. Great judges and great courts distinguish between the fundamental and the casual. They make the law to grow not by changing it, but by adapting it, with an understanding of the progress in our civilization, to new social conditions. It is the judges who are not grounded in the science of the law, and who have not the broad statesmanlike view that comes from its wide study, that are staggered by narrow precedent and frightened by technical difficulty. The decisions of courts criticised for a failure to respond to that progress in settled public opinion which should affect the limitations upon the police power, or the meaning of due process of law, have generally been rendered by elected courts. Paradox as it may seem, the appointed judges are more discriminatingly responsive to the needs of a community and to its settled views than judges chosen directly by the electorate, and this because the Executive is better qualified to select greater experts.

More than half a century's experience with the election of judges has not, therefore, commended it as the best method, though, for the reasons stated, its results up to this time are better than might have been expected. But with the changes proposed in the manner of making nominations and of conducting elections of judges the system is certain to become less satisfactory. Now we are to have no state or county or district conventions, and the judges are to be nominated by a plurality in a popular primary, and to be voted for at the election on a non-partisan ticket, without party emblems, or anything else to guide the voter. Like all the candidates for office to be elected under such conditions, they are expected to conduct their own canvass for their nomination, to pay the expenses of their own candidacy in the primary, and in so far as any special effort is to be made in favor of their nomination and election, they are to make it themselves. They are necessarily put in the attitude of supplicants before the people for preferment to judicial

places. Under the convention system it happened
not infrequently, for reasons I have explained,
that men who were not candidates were nominated
for the Bench, but now in no case can the office
seek the man. Nothing could more impair the
quality of lawyers available as candidates or
depreciate the standard of the judiciary. It has
been my official duty to look into the judiciary of
each State in my search for candidates to be
appointed to Federal judgeships, and I affirm
without hesitation that in States where many of
the elected judges in the past have had high rank,
the introduction of nomination by direct primary
has distinctly injured the character of the Bench
for learning, courage and ability. The nomination and election of a judge are now to be the
result of his own activity and of fortuitous circumstances. If the judge's name happens to be
the first on the list, either at the primary or the
election, he is apt to get more votes than others
lower down on the list. The incumbent in office,
because he happens to be more widely known,
has a great advantage. Newspaper prominence
plays a most important part, though founded on
circumstances quite irrelevant in considering
judicial qualities.

The result of the present tendency is seen in the
disgraceful exhibitions of men campaigning for

the place of State Supreme Judge and asking votes, on the ground that their decisions will have a particular class flavor. This is the logical development of the view that a popular election is the only basis for determining right and justice; but it is so shocking, and so out of keeping with the fixedness of moral principles which we learned at our mother's knee, and which find recognition in the conscience of every man who has grown up under proper influence, that we ought to condemn without stint a system which can encourage or permit such demagogic methods of securing judicial position. Through the class antagonism unjustly stirred up against the Courts, fiery faction is now to be introduced into the popular election of judges. Men are to be made judges not because they are impartial, but because they are advocates; not because they are judicial, but because they are partisan.

It is true that politics have played a part even when judges have been appointed. They have usually been taken from the lawyers of the prevailing party. The President or a Governor appointing them has been elected on a partisan ticket, is the titular head of his party, and is expected to give preferment to those who supported him. This has not, however, resulted in political courts, because the control of the Gov-

ernment has naturally changed from one party
to another in the course of a generation and has
normally brought to the Bench judges selected
from both parties; and then, if the judges are
made independent by the character of their
tenure, the continued exercise of the judicial
function entirely neutralizes in them any possible
partisan tendency arising from the nature of
their appointment.

More than this, there is a noticeable disposition
on the part of some Chief Executives to disregard
party in making judicial appointments, and this
ought to be so. In the early history of our
country, and indeed down to the Civil War, the
construction of the Constitution as to the powers
of the Federal Government was a party question,
and doubtless affected the selection of Federal
Judges. Yet the effect of the judgments of Marshall and his Court was not weakened by Taney
and his Democratic associates when they came to
consider the Constitution. The Federalist party
died in 1800, but its national view of our Government was vitalized by John Marshall, and preserved by the Supreme Court in unchanged form
until the Civil War robbed the States' rights issue
of its political and sectional importance. To-day
a sound and eminent lawyer of either party, who
can conscientiously take the oath to support the

Constitution, may be appointed by a conscientious
Executive. What is true of the National Government is true of the State governments, and there
is not the slightest reason why an Executive should
not appoint to the judiciary of his State qualified
persons from either party.

I come now to consider what should be the
judicial tenure of office. In our Federal and
State constitutions the rights of the individual
as against the aggression of a majority of the
electorate, and, therefore, against the Government itself, are declared and secured in a way
peculiar to our Anglo-Saxon ancestors. The
abstract declarations in favor of personal liberty
and the right of property in the fundamental law
of the continental countries were often as ample
as in ours, but it was in the provision for the
specific procedure to secure them that the early
English charters of freedom, the Magna Charta,
the Petition of Right and the Bill of Rights, were
remarkable. This procedure is preserved in our
constitutions and, upon the initiative of the individual who conceives his rights infringed, is to be
invoked in the courts. Therefore, the first requisite of the judiciary is independence of those
branches through the aggression of which the
rights of the individual may be impaired. The
choice of the judges must always rest either in a

majority of the electorate of the people, or in a popular agent whom that majority selects, and so must be directly or indirectly in control of the party to be charged in such controversies with the infringement of individual rights. How, therefore, can we secure a tribunal impartial in recognizing such infringements and courageous enough to nullify them? It is only by hedging around the tenure of the judges after their selection with an immunity from the control of a temporary majority in the electorate and from the influence of a partisan Executive or legislature.

Our forefathers who made the Federal Constitution had this idea in their minds as clear as the noonday sun, and it is to be regretted that in some of their descendants and of the successors in their political trust this sound conception has been clouded. They provided that the salaries of the judges should not be reduced during their terms of office, and that they should hold office during good behavior, and that they should only be removed from office through impeachment by the House of Representatives and a trial by the Senate. The inability of Congress or of the Executive, after judges have been appointed and confirmed, to affect their tenure has given to the Federal judiciary an independence that has made it a bulwark of the liberty of the individual. On the other hand, this immunity has had some effect in making Congress grudge any betterment of the compensation to these great officers of the law. Congress has failed to recognize the increased cost of living as a reason for increasing judicial salaries, although this fact has furnished the ground for much other legislation. They have declined to conform the income of the judges to the dignity and station in life which they ought to maintain, and have kept them at so low a figure as to require from that class of lawyers who are likely to furnish the best candidates for judicial career a great pecuniary self-sacrifice in accepting appointment. I presume, therefore, that in spite of the efforts of the Bar and of men of affairs to increase judicial salaries, and in spite of the confession as to the cost of living in Washington that actual service in the Government wrings from the advocates of a simple life who happen to get into office, we must continue to require from those who have the honor, the responsibility and the labor of the exercise of judicial functions under the Federal Government, mean living and high thinking, and we must endure the indignation that is justly stirred in us when widows and children of men, able and patriotic, who have served their country faithfully and have done enormous labor for two or three decades on the Bench, are left without sufficient means to live. Nothing but the life tenure of the Federal judiciary, its independence and its power of usefulness have made it possible, with such inadequate salaries, to secure judges of a high average in learning, ability and character.

When judges were only agents of the King to do his work, it was logical that they should hold office at his pleasure. Now, when there is a recrudescence of the idea that the judge is a mere agent of the sovereign to enforce his views as the only standards of justice and right, we naturally recur to the theory that judges should hold their office at the will of the present sovereign, to wit, the controlling majority or minority of the electorate. The judicial recall is a case of atavism and is a retrogression to the same sort of tenure that existed in the time of James I, Charles I, Charles II and James II, until its abuses led to the act of settlement securing to judges a tenure during their good behavior. It is argued that there is no reason to object to a recall of judges that does not apply to judges elected for a term of years. The answer is that the conceded objections to an elective judiciary holding for a short term of years are doubled in force in their application to judicial recall. The States which have elective judges have gotten along somehow through the political capacity of the American people and the force of public opinion to make almost any system work. Under the present system a judge is certain to retain his position for a few years, and during that time at least he is free from interruption or the threat of popular disapproval. This certainty of tenure, though short, conduces to the independent administration of his office. As he draws near another election and hopes to have another term, it is true that his courage and his impartial attitude toward issues that have any political bearing are likely to be severely tested. Because the country has survived a judiciary largely selected in this manner does not seem to be a very strong reason why we should proceed to increase the evil effect of the short tenure by making it merely at the will of the plurality of those of the electorate who choose to vote.

I have stated my reasons for thinking that appointment of judges results in the selection of better experts in the science of law than the elective system. But even if the qualifications of the two incumbents under the two systems were equal upon their accession to office, the longer experience afforded by the life tenure and the greater opportunity it gives to learn the judicial duties make the better average judges. It matters not how experienced a man may be in the learning of the law, and in its practice, there are still lessons before him which he must learn before he can become of the greatest public service.

Other benefits from the life tenure in its effect upon the judges who enjoy it are that it makes the incumbents give their whole mind to their work, to order their household with a view to always being judges, and to take vows, so to speak, as to their future conduct. They must put aside all political ambition. One of the great debts which the American people owe to Mr. Justice Hughes is the example that he set in the last presidential election when the most serious consideration was being given to making him the candidate of the Republican party. He announced his irrevocable determination not to enter the political field because he had assumed the judicial ermine.

What, now, are the objections urged to a life tenure? The first is that it makes judges irresponsible, in the sense that they are so freed from the effect of what people think of them that they are likely to do unjust and arbitrary things. The immunity of life tenure does make some judges forget that it is nearly as essential to give the appearance of doing justice as it is to do substantial justice. They forget that the public must have confidence in, and respect for, the Courts in order that they achieve their highest usefulness in composing dangerous differences and securing tranquillity and voluntary acquiescence in the existing order. Still, the life judges in whom these faults really exist are comparatively few. The criticism is apt to be made in many cases where it is not deserved, because of the contrast that lawyers and litigants find in dealing with courts under the two systems. The Federal Judges have the power which the English judges have. They are so far removed from politics or the fear of election that the counsel before them receive only the consideration which their eminence as lawyers justifies. Under State statutes, following the tendency to minimize the power of the Court, the judge is greatly restricted in the exercise of discretion to free the issue before the Court from irrelevant and confusing considerations. The jury trial given by the Federal Constitution is the trial at common law given by a court and jury, in which the court exercises the proper authority in the management of the trial and assists the jury in a useful analysis and summing up of the evidence, and an expression of such opinions as will help the jury to reach right conclusions. All this tends to eliminate much of what almost might be called

demagogic discussion, which counsel are prone to
resort to in many of the local State Courts, and
which the State judge fears to limit lest it be
made the basis of error and a ground for new
trial under some statute narrowing his useful
power. We must, therefore, weigh the frequent
characterization of the Federal Judge as a petty
tyrant in the light of the contrast between proper
authority exercised by him and the control exercised by judges in State Courts, where opportunity is too frequently given to the jury to
ignore the charge of the court, to yield to the
histrionic eloquence of counsel, and to give a
verdict according to their emotions instead of
their reason and their oaths. Why is it that every
lawbreaker prefers to be tried in a State Court?
Why is it that the Federal Courts are the terror
of evildoers? One of the reasons may be found
in the better organization of the Federal prosecuting system. But is it not chiefly because the
judge retains his traditional control of the
manner of the trial and of the counsel and really
helps, but does not constrain, the jury to a just
verdict? Is it not because law and justice more
certainly prevail there rather than buncombe and
mere sentiment?

But it is said that the unpopularity of the
Federal Courts among the lawyers as a whole

shows that the life tenure has a bad effect upon their character as judges. I agree that when a judge is thoroughly disliked by the Bar, who are his ministers and assistants, it is generally his fault, because he has much opportunity properly to cultivate their good will and respect. Still, much must be allowed for in the impatience of the general Bar at Federal Judges, because there are many lawyers who appear but rarely in United States Courts, are embarrassed by their unfamiliarity with the mode of practice, and feel themselves in a strange and alien forum.

There are substantial causes for the local unpopularity of Federal Courts and these exist without any fault of the judges. The chief reason for creating local courts under the Federal authority was to give to non-residents an opportunity to have their cases tried in a court free from local prejudice before a judge who had the commission of the President of the whole country, rather than a judge whose mandate was that of the Governor of the State where the cause was tried, or of the people of the county in which the court was held. In other words, the very office which they serve, that of neutralizing local prejudice, necessarily brings them more or less into antagonism with the people among whom such local prejudice exists.

A similar answer may be made to the charge against the Federal Courts, that they are biased in favor of corporations. This has grown naturally out of their peculiar jurisdiction. Throughout the Western and Southern States, foreign capital has been expended for the purpose of development and in the interest of the people of those sections. They have been able to secure these investments on reasonable terms by the presence in their communities of the Federal Courts, where the owners of foreign capital think themselves secure in the maintenance of their just rights when they are obliged to resort to litigation. While this has been of inestimable benefit in rapid settlement and progress, it has not conduced to the popularity of the Federal Courts. Men borrow with avidity, but pay with reluctance, and do not look upon the tribunal that forces them to pay with any degree of love or approval.

Then, an important part of the litigation in the Federal Courts on the civil side consists of suits brought to prevent infringement by State action of the right of property secured by the Fourteenth Amendment to the Constitution. Such action is usually directed against large corporations, who thus become complainants. If any such suits are successful, and State action is enjoined, it is easy for the demagogue and the

muckraker to arouse popular feeling by assertion
that the Federal Courts are prone to favor corporate interests. It is not the bias of the judges,
but the nature of their jurisdiction, that properly
leads litigants of this kind to seek the Federal
forum. The unsuccessful suits of this kind are
never considered by the critics of the Federal
judiciary. Hence the plausibility of the charge.
But it is unjust. In no other courts have the
prosecution of great corporations by the Government been carried on with such success and such
certainty of judgment for the wrongdoer, and the
influence of powerful financial interests has had no
weight with the Federal Judges to prevent the
enforcement of law against them.

Again, the litigation between non-resident
railway and other corporations and their employees in damage suits has usually been removed
from the State Courts to the Federal Courts,
where a more rigid rule of law limiting the liability of the employer has been enforced. This has
created a sense of injustice and friction in local
communities that is entirely natural, and has
given further support to the charge that the
Federal Courts are the refuge of great corporations from just obligation. It was the business
of Congress to remove this by adopting an interstate commerce employers' liability act like that

which is now on the statute book, giving the
employees much fairer treatment, and by passing
the workman's compensation bill which is pending
in Congress and will, I hope, soon be enacted into
law.

But it is said, "When you get a bad judge you
cannot get rid of him under the life system."
That is true unless he shows his unworthiness in
such a way as to permit his removal by impeachment.   Under the authoritative construction by
the highest court of impeachment, the Senate of
the United States, a high misdemeanor for which
a judge may be removed is misconduct involving
bad faith or wantonness or recklessness in his
judicial action or in the use of his judicial influence for ulterior purpose.   The last impeachment
and removal of a Federal Judge, that of Judge
Archbald, was on the ground that he sought sales
of property from railroad companies, or their
subsidiary corporations, which were likely to be
litigants in his courts, and indicated clearly by
a series of transactions of this sort his hope and
purpose that such companies would be moved to
comply with his request because of his judicial
position.   The trial and the judgment were most
useful in demonstrating to all incumbents of the
Federal Bench that they must be careful in their
conduct outside of Court as well as in the Court

itself, and that they must not use the prestige of their judicial position, directly or indirectly, to secure personal benefit. Mr. Justice Chase was tried in Jefferson's time for gross improprieties of a partisan political character calculated to cast discredit on his Court. It would seem in this day and generation that he ought to have been removed, but the spirit of the impeachers was so partisan and political that it frightened many of the Senators and neutralized the improprieties that were made the subject of the impeachment articles. It was this case which evoked from Thomas Jefferson the comment that impeachment was "the scarecrow" of the Constitution, and that it was impracticable as a means of disciplining judges. Under the ruling in the Archbald case and the evident tendency of the Senate, the criticism of Jefferson has lost much of its force.

The procedure in impeachment is faulty, because it takes up the time of the Senate in long-drawn-out trials. This fact is apt to discourage resort to the remedy and has lessened its proper admonitory and disciplinary influence. The pressure upon both Houses for legislation is so great that the time needed for inquest and trial is grudgingly given. An impeachment court of judges has been suggested, but the public would fear in it lenity toward old associates. The wisdom of having the trial by the higher branch of the Congress, entirely free from the spirit of the guild, commended itself to the framers of the Constitution and is manifest. A change in the mode of impeachment, however, so as to reduce materially the time required of the Senate in the proceeding, would be of the greatest advantage. If the whole Senate were not required to sit in the actual trial, and the duty were remitted to a committee like the judiciary committee of that body, whose decision could be carried on review to the Senate in full session, the procedure might be much shortened. The Judicial Committee of the English Privy Council is now a supreme court for colonial appeals, probably having its origin in the difficulty of assembling the whole Council to attend to litigated causes. The English House of Lords is a court, but sits only with the Law Lords, who are really a judiciary committee of the Peers to act as such.

It has been proposed that instead of impeachment, judges should be removed by a joint resolution of the House and the Senate, in analogy to the method of removing judges in England through an address of both Houses to the King. This provision occurs in the Constitution of Massachusetts and in that of some other States, but it is very clear that this can only be justly done after full defense, hearing and argument. Professor McIlwain of Harvard has written a very instructive article on the subject of removal by address in England, in which he points out that this is a most formal method, and that in the only case of actual removal of a judge by this method a hearing was had before both Houses of Parliament quite as full, quite as time-consuming and quite as judicial as in the proceeding by impeachment. Advocates of the preposterous innovation of judicial recall have relied upon the method of removal of judges as a precedent, but the reference only shows a failure on the part of those who make it to understand what was the removal by address.

By the liberal interpretation of the term "high misdemeanor," which the Senate has given it, there is now no difficulty in securing the removal of a judge for any reason that shows him unfit, and if the machinery for holding the trial could be changed from the full Senate to a judicial committee, with the possible appeal to the whole body, impeachment would become a remedy entirely practical and effective.

One who is convinced that the Federal judiciary, both supreme and inferior, because they are appointed and hold office for life, are the greatest bulwark in the protection of individual right and individual liberty and the permanent maintenance of just popular government, must have a strong personal resentment against any member of that body who in any way brings discredit on the Federal judiciary and weakens its claim to public confidence. I feel, therefore, no leniency or disposition to save the Federal Judges from just criticism and I am far from making light of serious charges against them or of defects that have cropped out from time to time.

Some local Federal Judges are not sufficiently careful to avoid arousing local antagonism in cases where they have a choice as to the method of granting a suitor relief. Congress has taken steps in this direction so that one judge is not enough to authorize an injunction where it is sought to prevent the enforcement of a State statute claimed to violate individual rights.

Again, the patronage that judges have exercised has disclosed a weakness that can be prevented by changing the system. Judges now appoint clerks and the relation established between the judge and the clerk is so close and confidential that it is often difficult to secure from the judge the proper attitude of criticism toward the clerk's misconduct. I am convinced that the clerks ought to be appointed by the Executive, be brought within the classified civil service, and be subject to removal for cause either by the Executive or by the judge.

Abuses have grown out of court appointments to receiverships and to other temporary lucrative positions. It would be well if possible to relieve the judges of such duties. In the case of national banks, the receivers are appointed, not by the Courts, but by the Comptroller of the Currency. I think it might be well in the case of interstate railroads, the creditors of which seek relief in the Federal Court, to have the receivers appointed by the Interstate Commerce Commission. Patronage is very difficult to dispense. It gives to the Court a meretricious power and casts upon it a duty that is quite likely to involve the Court in controversies adding neither to its dignity nor its hold upon the confidence of the public. Some great English judges have tarnished their reputation in its use. A receiver appointed by another authority would be quite sufficiently under control of the Court if the Court could remove him for cause and punish him for contempt of its orders.

Again, the judges in the Federal Courts have not shown as strong a disposition as they should to cut down the expenses of litigation; but this is completely in the control of Congress, which would help the people much more by enacting a

proper fee bill than by such attempts as we have
seen, to impair the power of Courts to enforce
their lawful decrees. The attitude of the Federal
Courts as to the cost of litigation was originally
brought about by the increase in litigation and
the hope that heavy costs would operate as a limitation, but this works great injustice and is an
improper means to the end.

The great defects in the administration of justice in our country are in the failure to enforce
the criminal laws through delay and ineffective-
ness of prosecution in the criminal courts, and in
the cost and lack of dispatch in civil suits. In
the enforcement of the criminal laws of the United
States in the Federal Courts there is little to criti-
cise. They might well serve as models to the
State Courts. On the civil side, the same cannot
be said. The costs may be and ought to be
greatly reduced. The procedure in equity causes
has been greatly simplified by the new equity rules
just issued by the Supreme Court. A bill to
authorize that Court to effect the same result in
cases at law is likely soon to pass. Then we may
hope that the Federal Courts will furnish a complete object lesson to State legislatures in cheap,
speedy and impartial judgment.

I have thus taxed your patience with the
reasons that convince me that appointment and a

life tenure are essential to a satisfactory judicial system. They may seem trite and obvious, but I have thought in the present disposition to question every principle of popular government that has prevailed for more than a century, that it might be well, at the risk of being commonplace, to review them.

In the present attitude of many of the electorate toward the Courts, it is perhaps hopeless to expect the States, in which judges are elected for short terms, to return to the appointment of judges for life. But it is not in vain to urge its advantages. The Federal Judges are still appointed for life, and it will be a sad day for our country if a change be made either in the mode of their selection or the character of their tenure. These are what enable the Federal Courts to secure the liberty of the individual and to preserve just popular government.

IX

"To Establish Justice"—(Continued)

Public Need of Educated Lawyers and Judges

The Necessity and Advantage of Judge-Made Laws

A great French judge truly said that the profession of the law was "as old as the Magistrate, as noble as Virtue, and as necessary as Justice." The importance of having a Bar, the members of which are sufficiently skilled in the principles of law and the procedure of the Courts, properly to advise laymen as to their rights and the method of asserting or defending them, and to represent them in judicial controversies, I need not dwell upon. It has been the habit in many States to regard the practice of the law as a natural right, and one of which no one of moral character can be deprived. Such a view of course ignores the importance of the profession to society and looks at its practice only as a means of earning a living. Laymen can readily be made to see that society should be protected against the malpractice of the medical profession and surgery by men who know nothing of disease or the effect of medicine, or the handling of a surgical instrument. It is, therefore, comparatively free from difficulty to secure laws prescribing proper educational quali-fications for those holding themselves out as physicians or surgeons. The danger to society of the misuse of the power which a lawyer's pro-fession enables him to exercise is not so acutely impressed upon the layman until he has had some experience in following bad advice. A legal adviser can not ordinarily injure his client's bodily health, but he can lead him into great pecuniary loss and subject him and his family to suffering and want. The more thorough the general education of one who proposes to be a lawyer, the more certainly his mind will be dis-ciplined to possess himself of the principles of law and properly to apply them. There is a spirit of hostility manifested by some courts and lawyers, and some who are not lawyers, to the suggestion that a fundamental general education is necessary to the making of a qualified member of the legal profession. In Indiana the constitu-tion impliedly forbids the imposition of examina-tion for admission to the Bar. The argument is: "Look at Abraham Lincoln. He never had any education of any sort. He educated himself, and note his greatness both as a lawyer, a statesman

and a man." Such an argument would do away
not only with the necessity for education at the
Bar, but the necessity for school or colleges of
any kind. The question is not whether excep-
tional men have made themselves learned men,
educated men and great lawyers without the use
of schools, academies, colleges or law schools, but
the question is by what means are we likely to
produce the best average members of the profession. By what means are we most likely to make
them skilled and able and useful in the office for
which the profession is created? Certain law
schools in the country have imposed the necessity
for a collegiate education upon intending lawyers
before they shall begin the study of their profession. In the medical profession, schools of a similar standard require, after the Bachelor's degree,
a study of four years. In the law schools a study
of three years is now generally required, and in
many States the same period has been fixed as
the necessary period of preparation for the Bar
examinations. It is said this will exclude many
worthy young men who would aspire to the law.
As the reason of the profession for being is to
serve society, the interest of society is the point
from which we must approach the question, and
but little consideration should be given to the
welfare of those who would like to practice law

and are not fitted to do it well. The graduates of colleges are in number greatly more than sufficient to supply the needs of the clerical, the medical and the legal professions, and there is no danger that there will be any dearth of lawyers of good material because a heavier burden of preparation is required of them. The view that the profession exists solely as a livelihood creates a demand for law schools furnishing the easiest and shortest way for their students to acquire the temporary information needed to pass the required examinations. Such schools are cramming factories with no thought to the broad legal education which students should bring to the practice after they are admitted to the Bar. They confer only a smattering of the law and only a transient familiarity with the subjects upon which they are examined.   Men who are thus prepared may become good lawyers, but if they do, it will be because of their natural mental capacity and the education that they give themselves afterwards, and not because of any basis of legal learning they acquired in such schools. For the good of society, the standards of legal education ought to be made higher and a broad collegiate education before the study of the law should be insisted upon as the *sine qua non.*

In most States the question of the admission to

the Bar is given to the Supreme Courts. It should
be possible, therefore, to secure, through such
good and eminent lawyers, a proper standard for
the making of new lawyers. They ought, of all
men, to appreciate in the highest degree the
benefit in the administration of justice of requiring the most thorough preparation for the practice of the profession. They could impose a standard for preliminary and fundamental education,
and then for the education in law. Of course the
judges do not generally prepare the questions
for examination, or mark them. They delegate
this to a committee of lawyers. When we find
in one of the great States of the Union a committee of examination that imposed questions
based on cases taken from reports of its own
State, some of doubtful authority, and gave no
credit for answers which differed from the decisions of the Courts, however good the reasons, we
are not surprised to learn that some of the best
prepared students from first-class law schools
were rejected, and that applicants with education
in the law much less thorough were admitted. The
latter pursued the course of studying the special
character of previous questions and "cramming"
the answers to them from a book prepared by one
of the committee. This book shows not a few
instances in which the answers required were

hardly sustained by good authority, even in the particular State. Some features of this bad system have been changed. The reform should be more radical. No court that knowingly permits such a system to remain in vogue can escape criticism. Examinations of this kind commercialize the practice of the law more than any other one. Those who come to the Bar by a mere trick of memory, and without thorough absorption of legal principles, are not likely to improve the tone of the practice to which they have succeeded by such means.

What I wish to dwell upon especially here is the influence of a proper standard for admission to the Bar on another function of lawyers than that of advising and representing clients. We get our judges from the Bar, and we add to the education of our judges when they are on the Bench by the Bar. It is the tone of the Bar, therefore, and the ability and learning of the Bar that necessarily affect the learning and standards of the Bench. The influence of a great Bar to make a great court and to secure a series of great decisions, every one familiar with judicial history knows.

The function of judges is to interpret constitutions and statutes, and apply and enforce them, and also to declare and apply that great body of customary law known as common law which we

received from past generations. According to
the view and theory of one who does not understand the practical administration of justice,
judges should interpret the exact intention of
those who established the Constitution, or who
enacted the legislation, and should apply the
common law exactly as it came to them. But
frequently new conditions arise which those who
were responsible for the written law could not
have had in view, and to which existing common
law principles have never before been applied, and
it becomes necessary for the Court to make new
applications of both. The power which the Court
thus exercises is said to be a legislative power, and
it is urged that it ought to be left to the people.
That it is more than a mere interpretation of the
legislative or popular will, and in the case of the
common law that it is more than a mere investigation and declaration of traditional law is undoubtedly true. But it is not the exercise of
legislative power as that phrase is used. It is
the exercise of a sound judicial discretion in sup-
plementing the provisions of constitutions and
laws and custom, which are necessarily incomplete
or lacking in detail essential to their proper application, especially to new facts and situations constantly arising. Then, too, legislation is frequently so faulty in proper provision for con-

tingencies which ought to have been anticipated
that courts can not enforce the law without
supplying the defects and implying legislative
intention, although everyone may recognize that
the legislative body never thought anything
about the operation of the law in such cases and
never had any intention in regard to them.
Neither constitutional convention nor legislature
nor popular referendum can make constitutions
or laws that will fit with certainty of specifica-
tion the varying phrases of the subject matter
sought to be regulated, and it has been the office
of courts to do this from time immemorial.
Indeed, it is one of the highest and most useful
functions that courts have to perform in making
a government of law practical and uniformly
just. You can call it a legislative power if you
will, but that does not put you one bit nearer a
sufficient reason for denying the utility and
necessity of its exercise by courts.

Of all the people in the world who ought not to
be heard in objection are the advocates of the
initiative and referendum as a means of legislation. Legislatures and constitutional conventions have been bad enough in the enactment of
measures inconsistent in themselves, and full of
difficulty for those charged with their enforcement; but now it is proposed to leave the drafting

of laws to individual initiative and to submit them
to popular adoption without any possibility of
correction and needed amendment after discussion, which is always afforded in the representative
system. The puzzles in legislation now presented
to courts by this new method of making laws can
be better understood by reading some of the per-
spiring efforts of the Supreme Court of Oregon.
Instead of dispensing with courts, this purer and
directer democracy is going to force upon judicial tribunals greater so-called legislative duties
than ever. Of course legislatures and the people
have always the power to negative the future
application of any judicial construction of a constitution, or a law, or any declaration of a common law principle, by amendment or new law.

The practical impossibility of making laws that
are universally applicable to every case has
thrown upon the Courts the duty of supplying the
deficiency either by construction of written laws
or constructive application of the common law.
This discretion of courts is guided and limited
by judicial precedents. The precedents form a
body of law called judge-made law by those who
would attack it; but it is better to have judge-
made law than no law at all. Indeed the curative
and lubricating effect of this kind of law is what
has made our popular governmental machinery

work so smoothly and well. I can not refer at
length to the now much-mooted question of the
power of the Courts to refuse to recognize legislative acts which are beyond the permissible discretion of the legislature in construing its own
constitutional authority. I can only say that the
power has been exercised for one hundred and
twenty-five years and unless the Courts continue
to retain it, individual rights and every interest
of all the people will come under the arbitrary
discretion of a constantly changing plurality of
the electorate to be exercised by varying and
inconsistent decisions of successive elections.

But however necessary it is to entrust such
discretion to the Courts, we must recognize that
its existence is made the basis for a general
attack, by professed reformers of society, upon
our judicial system, and that this attack is finding much sympathy among the people. There
are good grounds for criticising our present
administration of justice in the lax enforcement
of the criminal law and in the high cost and lack
of dispatch in civil litigation.

These defects are not all chargeable to the
Courts themselves, by any means. The lax administration of the criminal law is due in a marked
degree to the prevalence of maudlin sentiment
among the people, and the alluring limelight in

which the criminal walks if only he can give a little sensational coloring to his mean or sordid offense. Then the State legislatures, responding perhaps to a popular demand, and too often influenced by shallow but for the time being politically influential members of our own profession, devise every means to deprive the Court of its power at common law to control the manner of trial and to assist the juries, but not to constrain them, to right conclusions. Codes of procedure of immense volume and exasperating detail keep litigants "pawing in the vestibule of justice" while the chance of doing real justice fades away. Then, too, unnecessary opportunity for appeals and writs of error and new trials is afforded by statute, and the litigant with the longest purse is given a great advantage. More than this, many questions that ought to be settled by administrative tribunals with proper authority have been thrust upon the Courts. This has had two effects. It involves the Courts in quasi-political and economic controversies which they ought not to be burdened with, and which necessarily expose them to criticism as being prejudiced. Second, it takes up the time of the Courts in executive matters and delays dispatch of legitimate judicial work. The creation of the interstate commerce commission, of State public utilities commissions, of boards of

conciliation and arbitration in labor controversies, of commissions for fixing compensation
for injured workmen, and of other executive
agencies for the determination of issues involved
in proper governmental regulation and exercise
of the police power, is lifting much from the
Courts. Then the American Bar Association and
many State associations are zealously and successfully working to induce legislatures and courts by
statute and rules to simplify procedure and make
it a vehicle of quick justice at little cost.

But the lax administration of the criminal law
and the cost and delay of civil litigation are not
the special objects of attack by social reformers.
Their fire is directed against what they call the
legislative power of the Courts that I have described. This they contend is now being exercised to defeat measures essential to true social
progress by reactionary judges. Let us trace out
the reasons for this antagonism and perhaps in
them we can find the true solution of the difficulty
so far as there is any real substance in their
complaint.

In the Federal Constitution there were embodied two great principles, first, that the Government should be a representative popular
government, in which every class in society, the
members of which have intelligence to know what

will benefit them, is given a voice in selecting the representatives who are to carry on the Government and in determining its general policy. On the other hand, the same Constitution exalts the personal rights and opportunities of the individual and prescribes the judicial machinery for their preservation, against the infringement by the majority of the electorate in whose hands was placed the direction of the executive and legislative branches of the Government. The common law rule was followed, by which each individual was given independence in his action, so long as that independence did not infringe the independence of another. This has given the motive for labor, industry, saving and the sharpening of intellect and skill in the production of wealth and its re-use as capital to increase itself. The material expansion of our country, unprecedented in history, would have been utterly impossible without it. When the Constitution was adopted, there was not only legal independence of the individual, but actual independence in his method of life, because he could and did produce almost everything that was needed for his comfort in the then standard of living. We have now become a people with an immense urban population, far from the sources of necessary supply, and, therefore, we have become far more dependent on each other that life may go on and be enjoyed. While it is undoubtedly true that the living of the average individual is far more comfortable than it ever was, we have now reached a point in the progress of our material development when we are stopping to take breath and to make more account of those who are behind in the race. We are more sensitive to the inequality of conditions that exist among the people and the enjoyment of the comforts of life. We are pausing to inquire whether, by governmental action, some changes can not be made in the legal relations between the social classes, and in the amelioration of oppressive conditions affecting those who in the competition between individuals under existing institutions are receiving least advantage from the general material advance. It is essential that our material expansion should continue, in order to meet the demands of the growing population and to increase the general comfort. Were we to take away the selfish motive involved in private property we would halt, stagnate and then retrograde, the average comfort and happiness in society would be diminished, and those who are now in want would be poorer than ever. The trend of those who would improve society by collectivist legislation is toward increasing the functions of government, and one of the great difficul-

ties they have to meet is provision for the rapidly
increasing pecuniary burden thus entailed. Mu-
nicipalities and States which have attempted something of this kind are finding that their credit is
exhausted and their tax resources insufficient.
Whatever the changes, therefore, we must maintain, for the sake of society, our institutional
system of individual reward, or little of the progress so enthusiastically sought can be attained.
It is not alone constitutional restraints which
limit thoughtless, unjust and arbitrary popular
excesses, but also those of economic laws and the
character of human nature, and these latter work
with seemingly cruel inevitableness which ought to
carry its useful lesson home.

The social reformers contend that the old legal
justice consisted chiefly in securing to each individual his rights in property or contracts, but
that the new social justice must consider how it
can secure for each individual a standard of living and such a share in the values of civilization
as shall make possible a full moral life. They
say that legal justice is the removal of all those
restrictions on the free action of an individual
which are not necessary for securing the like
freedom on the part of his neighbors, while social
justice is the satisfaction of every one's wants so
far as they are not outweighed by others' wants.

The change advocated by the social reformers is really that the object of law should be social interests and not individual interests. They unjustly assume that individual rights are held inviolate only in the interest of the individual to whom such rights are selfishly important and not because their preservation benefits the community. On the contrary, personal liberty, including the right of property, is insisted upon because it conduces to the expansion of material resources which are plainly essential to the interests of society and its progress. We must continue to maintain it whether our aim is individualistic or social. As long as human nature is constituted as it is, this will be true. When only altruistic motives actuate men, it may be different.

But we must recognize the strong popular interest in the sociological movement and realize the importance of giving it a practical and successful issue. We are not tied to the defects of the past, or present, and we ought to be anxious to guide the proposed reforms so that we shall secure all the good possible from them without ignoring the inestimable boon of experience we have inherited from centuries of struggle toward better things.

The Supreme Court of the United States has given many evidences of its appreciation of the

changes in settled public opinion in respect to
the qualification of individual rights by the needs
of society. Its definition or rather lack of definition of the police power, and its proposed
method of pricking out its limitations in accord
with predominant public opinion, is an example.
Indeed, many other instances of the infusion of
social ideas into the law by construction of remedial statutes and by adjustment of common law
principles to cases of social justice could be cited.
It is noteworthy that this is most evident in the
highest of our Courts with judges of greatest
experience, ability and learning in fundamental
jurisprudence and of statesmanlike constructive
faculty. It is through discrimination and far-
sighted legislators and through great and learned
judges that we can safely and surely achieve the
social changes and reforms within the practical
range of enforceable law. It must be remembered that with men as they are, government and
law can not make every change in society however
desirable. Law which is unenforceable or ineffec-
tive is worse than none. There are zones in the
field of social relations in which progress can only
be made by the moral uplift of the individual members of society, and in which the use of legal
compulsion is worse than futile.

Nevertheless, many who are infused with the

new ideas are prone to look askance upon what they call the individualistic system and are quite willing to do away with the constitutional restraints and the teachings and influence of the common law upon which such a system must rest. Relying upon the willingness of an inflamed majority to possess themselves of advantages over a minority, or the individual, they advocate remedies that tend toward confiscation.

Attempts made to carry out such ideas have, of course, startled the owners of property and capital to measures of defense and leading members of the Bar have ranged themselves in support of these measures. Indeed, in the enormous material development, the services of the profession have been invoked and often to protect methods that were indefensible. The profession has suffered from not having that independence of clients, enjoyed by English barristers, in which the relation between the two is temporary and but for a single cause. Such a relation does not produce that widespread, popular impression of complete identity of the professional advocate and adviser with the client, especially the corporate client and all its interests and plans. For these reasons our profession at present is under suspicion of being subsidized by our relation to the property of our clients, and of not being able to discuss without prejudice the betterment of present conditions in society. Those who are advocating these reforms propose, therefore, in the future largely to dispense with lawyers, largely to dispense with constitutional restraints and to place their whole confidence in the direct action of the people, not only in the enactment of laws, not only in their execution and enforcement, but also in the judicial function of determining justice in individual cases. This hostility to our profession, while it is natural and can be explained, is unjust. We are as intelligent, generous, patriotic, self-sacrificing and sympathetic a class as there is in society. We are not opposed to progress, real progress. Moreover, we know how to do things, and in the end no successful legal step forward will be made without our aid and shaping. We are far from lacking in a desire to improve social conditions. We recognize the inequalities existing between social classes in our communities, and agree to the necessity of new legal conceptions of their duties toward each other. But we have been driven by circumstances into an attitude of opposition. The proposals made for progress have been so radical, so entirely a departure from all the lessons of the past and so dangerous to what we regard as essential in preserving the inestimable social advances we have made since the Christian era, that we have been forced to protest. The result is that at present the militant social reformers and the lawyers are far apart. We don't talk exactly the same language. It is enough to answer our expressed opinions for them to say that we think and talk as lawyers.

What, then, is it necessary for us to do in this coming crisis; for it is a crisis in the life of courts and administration of justice. Many of the social reformers are oblivious of the lessons to be derived from experience in enforcement and operation of laws upon society. They do not realize the necessity for making the many different rules of law fit a system that shall work. They bring to the repair of a mechanism of interlocking parts, rude and unsuitable instruments. Nothing could more reflect upon their crude conception of judicial procedure than the proposition of a recall of judicial decisions. Social changes are not to be successfully made by a cataclysm, unless present conditions are as oppressive as those which caused the French Revolution. To be valuable they must come slowly and with deliberation. They are to be brought about by discriminating legislation proceeding on practical lines and construed by courts having an attitude of favor to the object in view.

I have spoken little to my purpose if I have not

made clear the necessity for broadening much the qualification of the general body of our judiciary to meet the important and responsible requirements that the present crisis in our community has thrust upon them. Their coming duties call for a basic knowledge of general and sociological jurisprudence, an intimate familiarity with the law as a science, and with its history, an ability to distinguish in it the fundamental from the casual, and constructive talent to enable them to reconcile the practical aspirations of social reformers with the priceless lessons of experience from the history of government and of law in practical operation. How can this be brought about? Only by broadening the knowledge and studies of the members of the legal profession. It is they who make the judges, who contribute to their education, and who help them to just, broad and safe conclusions.

What we lawyers need now is to rouse our profession to speak out. We must be heard in defense of the good there is in our present society and in pointing out the social injury which a retrograde step may involve. But we must also put ourselves more in touch with the present thinking of the people who are being led in foolish paths. We must study sociological jurisprudence. We must be able to understand the attitude of the sociological reformer. We must show our sympathy with every sincere effort to better things. What the people need in respect to this matter is light, and the profession engaged in administering law, and in promoting just judicial conclusions, must contribute their valuable assistance in giving it. In so far as the conditions in society are new, in so far as its needs are different from what they seemed to be at the time of the adoption of the Constitution, or as they were recognized under the common law, embodied in a century of our judicial decisions, they should be studied by the profession. We should seek to know exactly what are the conditions that are sought to be remedied. We should be willing to meet them in seeking to remedy every condition that is possible to remedy consistently with the maintenance of those principles that are essential to the pursuit of material progress and the consequent attainment of spiritual progress in society and to permanent popular and peaceful government of law.

The working of the problem presented is not the task of a year. It may require a generation or more. We must prepare our successors, the future American Bar, to meet the demand.

Every law school should require those who are to be admitted to its halls to have a general education furnishing a sufficiently broad foundation upon which to base a thorough legal education. That general education ought to include a study of economics and a study of sociology, and the curriculum of every law school should include a close study of the science of general and sociological jurisprudence as a basis for the study of the various branches of our law; and this raising of law school standards should meet a sympathetic response from Supreme Courts in requirements for admission to the Bar. Then the members of the Bar will come to the discussion of social remedies in courts, in the halls of Congress and in legislatures, and in appeals to the people, properly equipped, and will bring the controversy down to a practical issue and the fight can be fought out on a common ground. The valuable lessons of the past will be given proper weight and real and enduring social progress will be attained. We shall avoid, then, radical and impractical changes in law and government by which we might easily lose what we have gained in the struggle of mankind for better things.

X

"To Insure Domestic Tranquillity, Provide for the Common Defense"

The next two purposes stated in the preamble for ordaining and establishing the Constitution were to "insure domestic tranquillity" and "provide for the common defense."

The Constitution gives to Congress the power to provide for calling forth the militia to execute the laws of the Union, suppress insurrections and repel invasions; to raise and support armies; to provide and maintain a navy.

Power is vested in the President, on application of the legislature of a State, or of the executive (when the legislature can not be convened) to protect it against domestic violence.

The President has direction of the foreign policy of the country, except when treaties are to be made, in which case the Senate, by a vote of two-thirds present, must concur in them, and except when foreign war is to be the policy, when Congress must declare it.

I shall devote this chapter to the consideration of the necessity for the maintenance of a national militia, an army and navy, and to the questions arising in respect to them, together with the possibility of avoiding war and securing peace and thus maintaining a common defense through our treaty-making power.

Save in the District of Columbia, and in the territories, under the exclusive jurisdiction of the Federal Government, domestic tranquillity is secured by the State authorities, and this by the municipal police in cities, by the sheriffs and constables in counties, and if these local arms are insufficient, by the State militia, acting under the direction of the Governor. The State authorities, as we have seen, may, however, invoke the assistance of the President of the United States through a formal notice to him that domestic violence prevails to such an extent that with their available forces they can not suppress it. Thereupon, the President of the United States in the discharge of his duty should order the army of the United States to the assistance of the State authorities in the maintenance of order.

But it is not essential for the use of the army of the United States to maintain order anywhere within the United States that the Governor or the legislature of the State should call upon the President for assistance. There is "a peace of the state," and there is "a peace of the United States." Obstruction to the laws of the State by force violates the peace of that State. Obstruction by force to the laws of the United States violates the peace of the United States, and the Supreme Court has specifically declared, in a number of cases, that there is a peace of the United States which it is the business of the President to preserve by all the force at his disposal. For instance, it is the duty of the Government, under the Constitution and the laws of the United States passed in accordance therewith, to circulate the mails. Now, if those mails are obstructed by violence, it is the duty of the President, by the United States marshal and his deputies, if they have sufficient force, to clear the obstructions and see to it that the agents of the Government in the mail service have freedom to discharge their functions. The same thing is true as to the enforcement of the orders and judgments of the United States Courts. Should the marshals and their deputies and the *posse comitatus*, whom the marshal is able to summon, be insufficient, then the President, pursuing certain preliminaries required under the statute, may direct the army to preserve the peace of the United States by enforcing the law of the United States.

This last phase of the Federal power was more often in evidence when there were Federal election laws regulating the holding of Congressional elections. It then became the duty of the President to direct the marshals to assist in the enforcement of those laws whenever their operation was obstructed, and even the army was at times called in for this purpose, until there was a rider on an appropriation bill, passed in the days of President Hayes, by which it was forbidden to use the army as a *posse comitatus*. I have always thought that this was a congressional limitation upon the executive power of doubtful constitutional validity.

This suggests the controversy between President Cleveland and Governor Altgeld as to the President's right to send troops to Chicago at the time of the so-called Debs strike and attempted rebellion against organized government. There the orders of the Federal Courts enjoining interference by large bodies of men with the operation of railways, and the obstruction of mails, were held for naught and were violently resisted by rioters, and President Cleveland, under the advice of Attorney-General Olney, and through the orders of Lieutenant-General Schofield, sent out Federal troops to Chicago under General Miles to see to it that these obstructions ceased. They were sent to preserve not the peace of Illinois but the peace of the United States. Governor Altgeld insisted that he had control of the situation, and that it was a usurpation on the part of President Cleveland to attempt to send Federal forces into his State. President Cleveland declined to recognize Governor Altgeld's right to object to his sending the troops of the Government in the United States wherever he might choose. He told the Governor that he did not have to wait for a request by the legislature of Illinois or by Governor Altgeld before he could, by use of the army, suppress unlawful obstruction to the laws of the United States or the process of its Courts.

The injunctions issued in the case against Debs were sustained as valid by the Supreme Court of the United States in a *habeas corpus* suit brought to release Debs from his imprisonment for contempt for defying those injunctions. In that case the Supreme Court, by unanimous judgment, left no doubt whatever that President Cleveland was entirely right in his action and that Governor Altgeld was much too narrow in his view of the power of the Federal Government in such a case.

The army of the United States is theoretically composed of three branches. First, there is the regular army of the United States. That to-day can not by law exceed 100,000 men, and its number is fixed by executive order of the President. Practically Congress must consent to the number because it appropriates money for the pay of the army. Its exact number, exclusive of about 4,000

Philippine Scouts, on June 30, 1913, was 4,665
officers and 75,321 men.   This is an army raised
by voluntary enlistment, in which the term of
enlistment is for seven years, with an obligation
on the part of the enlisted man to serve four years
with the colors and three years in the reserve,
during which in time of exigency he may be sum-
moned to active service.   Second, in addition to
the regular army of the United States, the
statutes provide for a so-called volunteer army of
the United States, an army raised only in time of
war.   It was the volunteer army that made up the
bulk of our great army during the Civil War.
Strictly speaking, this is no more a volunteer
army than is the regular army, because both are
the result of voluntary enlistments, but as the
volunteer army is only used in time of war and
the term is generally for a period limited by the
end of the war, it is supposed to embrace those
who but for the war would not enlist, while the
men of the regular army enlisted in time of peace
are considered professional or regular soldiers.

The present volunteer law is an old one, quite
inadequate to modern needs and especially defec-
tive in its provision that the officers of the volunteer army shall be appointed by the State Governors rather than by the President of the United
States.   When it became necessary to raise addi-

tional troops to secure tranquillity in the Philippine Islands, and a volunteer army of 30,000 men had to be raised, a special law was passed which placed the appointing power in the hands of the President. The men under this special act were enlisted for two years, and at the end of the two years, the regiments were as well trained as those of the regular army; but the special law expired by its own limitation, and now the old law remains in force. Effort after effort has been made to pass a new one, which would be ready for use should war threaten, so that the Executive, without waiting for new legislation, might at once raise a volunteer force. But the lingering States' rights prejudice in Congress and the apparent indisposition to part with the State political power, which the transfer of the appointment of officers in the volunteer force from the Governors to the President would involve, have thus far blocked the adoption of the new law.

Colonel Upton, an officer of the United States Army, and a great military authority, who wrote a very valuable book on the military policy of the United States, denounced the feature of our policy by which the State authorities are given power to appoint officers in the volunteer force as producing some of the most lamentable results in our military campaigns.

The third national force is the militia, called
the National Guard. The militia is a military
force raised under the State laws which the
National Constitution recognizes. It gives Congress authority to aid in the organization of the
militia, and to provide rules for its discipline and
drill. The President is its Commander-in-Chief
when it is acting under his call. Its function as a
national force is limited to the resistance to invasions of the national territory and it could not be
employed as a national force beyond the limits of
the United States in a foreign expedition.

This limit upon the national use of the National
Guard was made prominent in the Spanish War
when the question arose as to whether the famous
Seventh Regiment of New York should go to
Cuba. It very properly declined to tender its
organization for foreign service because the contract of enlistment by its men embraced only
domestic service; but every one of its members was
given full permission to enter any regular or
volunteer regiment for the war and many of them
went.

The chief function and the most frequent use
of the militia are in the maintenance of order in
the State under whose authority it is organized.
Unlike the volunteer army of the United States,
its officers should, therefore, be appointed by the

Governor, and so the Federal Constitution requires.

The people of the United States on the whole are a shrewd, enterprising and provident people, but they have not proven it by their military policy. Any one who is at all interested may have the utter foolishness and stupidity of that policy shown to them as clearly as the light of day by reading what I have already referred to, Colonel Upton's "History of the Military Policy of the United States." He shows from the beginning how, through the interference of political theories and the variation of different administrations, we have been ludicrously unprepared for wars into which we entered with all the confidence and non-chalance of a nation with a thoroughly equipped and adequate army. In the War of 1812 our regular army amounted to 6,000 troops. There were 5,000 British troops in Canada. Had we had an army of 25,000 at the time, we could have taken Canada without difficulty. Instead of that we suffered a number of humiliating defeats in the outset of the war and, before we finished it, we had upon paper enlisted in the army and paid for at one time or at another 500,000 troops. We have expended $50,000,000 in pensions paid for service in that war. The same thing is true of all of our wars, and Congress continues to be as reluctant as possible to maintain an adequate army to accomplish the legitimate purposes of such a force. So far as our military policy is concerned, it would seem as if the maxim that "The Lord looks after children and drunken men" ought to be extended to the United States, for by hook or crook, through mistakes of the enemy or through luck and by the expenditure of far greater treasure and many more lives than were necessary, we have generally been successful. This result is always used as an argument to resist a reasonable addition to the army and to incurring reasonable expense in time of peace that we may be better prepared in time of war. Men rise in their seats in Congress and pay deserved tributes to the bravery and efficiency of that volunteer army of half a million men who marched down Pennsylvania Avenue in the spring of '65 after the Civil War, and then point to them as a proof that we could organize an army of citizen soldiers in any emergency entirely adequate to meet foreign attack. They seem oblivious to the fact that it took three solid years of the hardest kind of practical training in actual warfare to make those citizen soldiers what they were—the best-trained army that ever trod in shoe leather. No standing army ever had a better training than they had. To use them as evidence that citizen soldiery can be whipped into an effective military force in the time in which effective and well-equipped European armies could be mobilized for action is to fly in the face of all reason and experience. Of course, our separation by oceans from possible enemies gives us the greatest good reason for avoiding the burdens and inconveniences of a large standing army, but we ought not for that reason to be helpless. We are very much nearer to Europe and Asia by many days than we were in Washington's time.

We are now policing the Philippines with about 12,000 of our troops. We are policing Hawaii with about 2,500 of our troops. We shall police the Isthmus with perhaps 3,000 of our troops. A force is necessary in Alaska, and in addition to these territories, we have between the oceans forty-eight States with a population of 90,000,000 people.

You may remember the controversy between Great Britain and this country over the boundary between Venezuela and British Guiana when President Cleveland demanded that the issue be arbitrated and Secretary Olney as Secretary of State asserted with startling abruptness the Monroe Doctrine and the intention of the Government of the United States to enforce it. The only other time when we came nearer to a breach with Great

Britain in the century of peace that has followed the War of 1812 was during the Civil War over the Trent affair. When we were taking this defiant position on the Venezuelan question, there was not on our whole coast a single fortification that could resist the guns of a modern navy. The then English fleet could have sailed into every important port of the United States and subjected every coast city to a ransom and been exposed to no danger except from one modern gun at Sandy Hook. The result of this informing experience was that the nation proceeded to defend itself by coastwise fortifications. And now as against a naval invasion, the country is very heavily fortified, but the guns of these fortifications need a force of some 40,000 men in order that every gun may be equipped with one complement of men.

We have spent upon these fortifications much more than $100,000,000. We are also fortifying the Philippine Islands by making Corregidor Island, which guards the entrance to Manila Bay, impregnable. We are fortifying Honolulu as a naval base and the defenses there will soon be formidable. We are fortifying the entrances to the Panama Canal and they soon will be swept by our guns in such a way that no naval attack can be made upon the canal. It is true that the coast fortifications in the United States proper are constructed with a view to resisting only a sea attack by navy and not a land attack by an army which might disembark at an unprotected point somewhere and march around to take the forts. This was a policy deliberately adopted in Mr. Cleveland's time, because it was not supposed that the prospect of the landing of a military force so far away from Europe, or so far away from Asia was a danger to be apprehended; but there is now being agitated the question whether this was not an error, and whether the fortifications ought not now to be supplemented in such a way that resistance could be made to land forces.

To-day the coast artillery, who are coast defense men, embrace upwards of 24,000 men. If you take this number from the 75,000 men we have in our army to-day, it leaves not more than 51,000 as a mobile army, and if you take from that number the 17,000 men that we use in the Philippines, Alaska, Hawaii and on the Isthmus of Panama, it leaves us in this country as the mobile army consisting of infantry, cavalry and light artillery, but 34,000 men. It is this force, amounting to about one in every 2,600 persons, that constitutes our regular army for use in the insurance of domestic tranquillity and the common defense of 90,000,000 people between the oceans.

This is not adequate for present legitimate
purposes. If the mobile army in the United States
were increased to 65,000, it would not be an exces-
sive provision. That would require an addition to
the army of 36,000. The passage of a proper
volunteer law is a crying need. I am glad to say
that the law with respect to the militia is a modern
law and has been improved by amendment from
time to time, and that the Federal Government is
intelligently spending money and exercising disciplinary authority to make a militia of 100,000
that could be called into requisition in time of a
war of defense.

One of the great difficulties that Presidents and
Secretaries of War now have in a proper management of the War Department is in the economical
and strategical housing of the troops in the
United States proper. An army of the size of ours
should be stationed at posts properly distributed
with a view to rapid concentration anywhere, but
few enough in number and large enough in capacity to permit the assembling at each post under
general officers, a large enough body of troops to
give the officers and men experience in drilling and
maneuvering with brigades and divisions instead
of with companies and battalions. In the Indian
Wars and for other reasons, the posts were
increased in number properly to meet the then

strategical necessities. Now four-fifths of them
ought to be abandoned to carry out the plan suited
to our present needs, and this is resisted for political reasons by members of Congress and the
Senate. A military post helps the neighborhood
because much government money is spent there
and the whole military policy of the United States
has to suffer from this political cause.

We may well take pride in such an army as we
have, for we have a body of army officers that
are brave, efficient and skilled, lacking in experience possibly in the mobilization and conduct of
great bodies of troops but as well educated in
military science as any officers in the world, and
as full of expedients and as adaptable to circumstances as any I know. We now have a general
staff of army experts to advise the Secretary of
War. It is impersonal and it insures the con-
tinuity of military policy so far as the War Department is concerned which makes for good.
Nevertheless, there is much to be done in order to
fit our army for its proper place in the discharge
of its constitutional functions and as a nucleus
and skeleton for the organization of an adequate
force, should war come upon us.

Now with respect to the navy, I only have to
say that until within recent times we had a navy
that made us third in the weight of our armament

and possibly second to Great Britain, but that now, with the number of keels laid down by other nations for new vessels, our rank is gradually being reduced. The laying down of two battle-ships a year would possibly have enabled us to keep a better position, but the failure of the last Congress and of this one to give us more than one battleship affects our future armament and of course our naval prestige. Farragut said that the best defense was well-directed fire against the enemy, and by the same reasoning a navy which is efficient to make your enemy fear its attack is one of the surest means of keeping your enemy's force out of your country.

The great objection to the maintenance of such an army and navy, as I have suggested, is the burden of its cost. Two hundred and fifty million dollars a year are necessary for this purpose, and this does not include the $150,000,000 or more that are devoted to pensions for those who were injured in the Civil War. Those pensions are not properly a part of the expense of the present mili-tary system of the United States, and ought not to play a part in determining the expenditures for our present army and navy. They are due to our not having had an adequate army ready in the past. Certain it is that the larger army and navy we maintain, the less in size will be our pension list after another war, should we have one, because the more adequate provision we make for a prompt and active campaign, the less men we shall enlist and the less their loss of life and limb.

When we compare our expenditures with those of the armies abroad, we see that the maintenance of a navy and an army is much more expensive to us per man than it is to the nations abroad. They have a conscription system while we depend on voluntary enlistment. We have to pay in money and support a living wage. They compel service practically without a wage in money. I have not the comparative figures for the cost of the European armies and our own this year, but in 1906 this statement which I made as Secretary of War was true:

"Our regular army to-day amounts in effective force to about 60,000 men, and it costs us in round numbers about $72,000,000 to sustain our military establishment. France maintains an army on the active list of 546,000 men, and it costs her $133,000,000. Germany maintains an army which has upon its active list 640,000 men, and it costs her $144,000,000 a year to maintain it. In other words, France has an army about nine times the size of ours which it costs her substantially less than twice the sum to maintain, while Germany has an army more than ten times as large which it costs her just about double our sum to maintain."

But you may say all this has a very military and warlike sound, coming from a man whose voice has been supposed to be for international peace, and if you charge me with inconsistency in this, you will only be repeating what has often been said against me for my advocacy of a more effective army and the maintenance of an adequate navy.

I am strongly in favor of bringing about a condition of securing international peace in which armies and navies may either be dispensed with or be maintained at a minimum size and cost; but I am not in favor of putting my country at a disadvantage by assuming a condition in respect to international peace that does not now exist and I am opposed to injuring the useful prestige and weight of her international influence which, under present conditions, an adequate army and an adequate navy are required to maintain.

I am as strongly in favor as any one can be of prosecuting every plan that will make war less and less probable. I believe there are practical plans that can accomplish much in this direction. I do not believe the plan of common disarmament is a practical plan. It has been tried and has failed. All Europe is an armed camp, and every time that any nation adds to its armament, the others with whom conflict is possible add to their respective armaments. Nothing but bankruptcy is going to stop these additions, and bankruptcy does not come as soon as we might properly welcome it.

The only thing that will bring about a disarmament is the certainty on the part of the nations, whose disarmament is important, that by some other means than war, they can secure the just and effective settlement of disputed questions that must arise between nations. When such a method is established and the nations are certain that it will accomplish its purpose, then they ought to have no motive for the maintenance of anything but a force sufficient to contribute to an international police force to carry out the decrees of the international tribunals in which international questions are settled.

I am an optimist, but I am not a dreamer, or an insane enthusiast on the subject of international peace. I realize the valuable uses to which wars have been put in the past and the progress that has been made through war in the civilization of the world. Resistance to tyrannical authority and despotism and the assertion of freedom have been possible only by revolution and the use of an armed force. Without such armed force, freedom

would not have been won and beneficent governments would not have been established.

We can count on peace as a result of the establishment of international tribunals only in as far
as the world is, or shall be, divided into nations
and countries under well-ordered and just governments which can enforce peace within their own
respective borders and prevent war of an inter-
necine or civil character.   As between nations,
with proper authority established within their own
borders, supported by the moral strength of their
own peoples, we can assume a proper basis for the
establishment of such international agreements as
may ultimately prevent international war.   Every
treaty that is made between two nations of this
established character, for the settlement of differences between them, by reference to an impartial
tribunal, is a step toward international peace.

But there is a long way before us in the accom-
plishment of our purposes upon this head.   And
meantime our country is occasionally subject to
the dangers that arise from the hostility of other
countries.   Since we have been a nation we have
been at war for one-fourth of the time, and, therefore, those who are responsible for the policy of
our Government have no right to assume that the
possibility of future wars has altogether ceased.

And this leads me to the question of the fortification of the Panama Canal. We built the Panama Canal to make another great avenue of trade for the world and to shorten the passage around Cape Horn and through the Straits of Magellan; but we also built it for our own national profit, first, in bringing the Pacific and Atlantic Coasts nearer together for the coastwise trade, and second, in developing the strategic efficiency of our navy in protection of our country, by offering a means of transferring the navy quickly from one seaboard to the other.

The proposition to neutralize the canal so that it shall always be open to every nation, whether we are at war with that nation or not, is to deprive us of that one very great advantage in using our navy to which I have referred, because while we could transfer our navy from one side to the other quickly through the canal, our enemy would enjoy the same strategical opportunity. Thus we would share with our enemy the advantage which we had planned and so lose it.

More than this, the canal is a very valuable property and the locks and machinery may be easily destroyed. Treaties of neutralization would not prevent a lawless nation from violating them and rendering useless to us the canal at a time of emergency when it is most necessary. We have the right to fortify the canal, given us by

Panama and acquiesced in by England, and there is not the slightest reason why we should not insure ourselves by fortifications against any injury which other nations may do.

The presence of fortifications does not lead us into war, and we don't have to use them unless there is some hostile threat against the canal. But it seems to me that we would be foolish in the extreme and utterly wanting in national prudence if we did not make it certain by our preparations that no nation can injure that work which has cost us $400,000,000 and which in time of national stress we shall certainly need. This is not at all inconsistent with the sincere desire never to have a war and to bring about peace as quickly as possible when we do have a war. It does not invite or approve a war any more than provision for a water supply invites or approves a conflagration. It is not at all inconsistent with the advocacy of treaties of arbitration and of general arbitration with all countries until those treaties are signed and until they embrace all nations of the earth, so that we can count on their effectiveness to prevent war.

We are thus naturally brought to the final topic of this chapter, and that is the treaties of general arbitration. We negotiated two of those treaties, one with France and the other with England. We then had so-called arbitration treaties with nearly all the nations of the world, but they excepted from their operation all questions of national honor or vital interest, and they provided that before they could become effective the Executive and the Senate of this country should make a special agreement with the country with whom we had the controversy for the special submission of the issues to the peace tribunal. These treaties, therefore, are practically nothing more than a general statement that we are in favor of arbitration of an issue when we agree to arbitrate it or, in other words, when we think it will be to our advantage to arbitrate it. Questions of national honor and of vital interest include all those questions, the agitation of which is likely to lead to war, and, therefore, arbitration treaties which except such questions may be said to be treaties for the settlement of those questions that never would involve war in their settlement anyhow. This clearly shows that they are not adapted at all to the purpose of preventing war.

The two treaties of peace we negotiated with France and Great Britain, however, took a decided step forward. First, they contained a formal agreement to submit either to The Hague, or to some other tribunal, all questions of difference arising between the two countries of a justiciable

character, and then they proceeded to define what
justiciable was by saying that it meant all questions that could be settled on principles of law or
equity. That certainly included questions of vital
interest and national honor, because they could
both be settled on such principles. Under the
second section, whenever a difference arose,
whether it was justiciable or not, of whatever kind, and negotiation could not settle it,
either party might delay final action for a year
by demanding an investigation of the difference
by a commission consisting of three persons
selected by one government and three persons by
the other to investigate and make a recommenda-
tion. If five of the commissioners decided that the
question was justiciable, in accordance with the
treaty, then both nations were bound to submit it
to its arbitration. It seems to me that the negotiation of such a treaty between France and the
United States, and between England and the
United States, and between the other nations of
Europe and the United States, would finally lead
to the negotiation of such treaties between European countries themselves, and ultimately that we
might have an interlacing and interlocking series
of treaties comprehending so many countries as to
lead to the formation of an international court of
judicature. Before this court, any nation being

aggrieved might bring any other nation to answer
its complaint, the case might be heard upon
proper pleadings and the judgment of the court
might be enforced either through the public
opinion of the nations, or, if that failed, through
an international police force. This may seem
an ambitious project and, as I have said, it is
essential to its carrying out that it be made between well-ordered governments which maintain
peace at home and within their own borders, and
which are sufficiently responsive to international
public opinion to fear its criticism and yield to its
demands. However remote such a court may be,
each treaty of this kind made would diminish the
chances of war, and when the system embraced all
governments, it would certainly make them more
willing to reduce armament and rely upon the
international court of judicature.

The treaties were defeated in the Senate. They
were defeated by amendments. One amendment
put in so many saving clauses as to the causes
which were to be arbitrated that it hardly seemed
worth while to offer such a truncated and nar-
rowed clause for reconsideration by the countries
with whom we had negotiated the treaties.

The Senators from the South were very sensitive
lest some of the repudiated debts of the Southern
States should be made the basis of international

arbitration by bondholders living in other countries. If these debts were just, they ought to be paid. If not, the tribunal would probably so decide. As a matter of fact, however, the treaties would not have included them because the language of the treaties only covered issues arising in the future, not past questions as these were.

The second and the chief objection to the treaty was that under its terms not only the Executive but the Senate was bound to arbitrate any difference which should be held, by five out of six of the commission established under the second clause, to be a justiciable one and therefore subject to arbitration. In other words, the Senate insisted that it could not agree to abide the decision of an international tribunal as to whether a treaty which it had entered into, bound it to submit to arbitration a certain question.

I never have been able to understand the force and weight of this argument. The Senate is not any more limited in its powers of agreeing to a treaty than the Executive. Both represent the Government. Now to say that this Government may not agree in advance with another government to arbitrate any of a class of questions that arises in the future, and to submit the question whether that issue is within the description of arbitrable questions as defined in the treaty, is to say that this Government has not any right to agree to do anything in the future. Such a limitation upon the treaty-making power of the Government and upon the treaty-making confirmation of the Senate is a limitation which would prevent this Government from entering into any useful arbitration treaty. It grows out of an exalted and unfounded idea by those who have for a long time been in the Senate, of the sacred nature of the Senate's function in treaty making as distinguished from the function of the Executive in making the same treaty which it has to confirm. A treaty binds the Government to some future action or else it is not a treaty at all. If a branch and agency of government has the treaty-making power, it has the right to bind the Government to something, and one of the commonest things that history has frequently illustrated as the subject of agreement is the submission of the construction of a treaty to an impartial tribunal. That is all this was. It was an agreement to submit to a tribunal the question whether the word "justiciable," as defined in the treaty, included an issue when that issue should arise.

But the treaties were defeated. Sometimes I have been very much disappointed, because I thought that their defeat was a retrograde step. Here we had two countries willing to go into a very comprehensive peace treaty with us of general arbitration, and after they were made, the Senate defeated the plan. If those nations could afford to make such treaties, why couldn't we do so? Have we any interests that could be prejudicially affected by such treaties more important to us than their interests could be to them? Is not the real objection to be found in the feeling on the part of many Senators that they are only in favor of arbitration when we can win and not when we may lose? That is not sincere support of the principle of arbitration.

Still I think the making of the general arbitration treaties and the discussion of them before the people have been useful, and that sometime in the future some other Executive may have the good fortune to negotiate another such treaty and to find a Senate not so sensitive as to its prerogative.

INDEX